Next Step GUIDED READING *in Action*

MW00535437

View & Do Guide

Jan Richardson

■SCHOLASTIC

ACKNOWLEDGEMENTS

Pioneer Valley Books and author Michèle Dufresne for graciously sharing Pioneer Valley Books resources and permitting us to use the following titles in these video lessons: *A Hungry Puppy* © 2006, *Super Dog* © 2010, and *Polar Bears* © 2011, all by Michèle Dufresne.

Many thanks to the staff and teachers at Belmont Elementary School, Prince William County Public Schools, Woodbridge, VA, who helped make this video resource possible.

Special thanks to:

Bridget Outlaw, Principal; Michelle Rowe, Title 1 PWCS Supervisor; Kathy O'Hara, Title 1 Professional Development Specialist; Angela Karch and Sarah Bayne, Reading Specialists; Judy Collazo, Krista Connor, Kelly Schultz, Jennifer Matice, Michelle Dunphy, and Katie Edmond, lead teachers.

CREDITS

Online Resources featured text and images:

PRE-A

Playing by Avelyn Davidson, illustrated by Jennifer Cooper. Copyright © 2009 by Weldon Owen. Published by Scholastic Inc.

EMERGENT

Let's Play by Catherine Peters, illustrated by Oksana Kemarskaya. Text copyright © 2009 by Scholastic Inc. Illustrations copyright © 2006 by Scholastic Canada Ltd. Published by Scholastic Inc.

Super Dog by Michèle Dufresne. Copyright © 2010 by Michèle Dufesne. Published by Pioneer Valley Books.

EARLY

A Hungry Puppy by Michèle Dufresne. Copyright © 2006 by Michèle Dufesne. Published by Pioneer Valley Books.

Little Red Riding Hood by Sara Shapiro, illustrated by Ellen Giggenbach. Copyright © 2009 by Weldon Owen. Published by Scholastic Inc.

TRANSITIONAL/FLUENT

The Great Gracie Chase by Cynthia Rylant, illustrated by Mark Teague. Text copyright © 2001 by Cynthia Rylant. Illustrations copyright © 2001 by Mark Teague. Published by Scholastic Inc.

Polar Bears by Michèle Dufresne. Copyright © 2011 by Michèle Dufresne. Published by Pioneer Valley Books.
All rights reserved.

COVER K–2: Photo © Nick Dolding/Getty Images.

Common Core State Standards copyright © 2010. National Governors Association Center for Best Practices and Council of Chief State School Officers. All rights reserved.

Managing Editor: Sarah Longhi
Content Editor: Sarah Glasscock
Coordinating Video Producer: Shelley Griffin
Video Production Services by Seed Multimedia, LLC. Producer/Director: Kevin Carlson
Assistant Video Producer and Copyeditor: Lynne Wilson
Interior Design: Brian LaRossa
Cover Design: Maria Lilja

Excepting those parts intended for classroom use, no part of this publication may be reproduced in whole or in part, or stored in a retrieval system, or transmitted in any form or by any means, electronic, mechanical, photocopying, recording, or otherwise, without written permission of the publisher. For information regarding permission, write to Scholastic Inc., 557 Broadway, New York, NY 10012. Scholastic Inc. grants teachers who have purchased Next Step Guided Reading in Action permission to reproduce from this book those pages intended for use in their classrooms. Notice of copyright must appear on all copies of copyrighted materials.

Copyright © 2013 by Jan Richardson.
All rights reserved. Published by Scholastic Inc.
Printed in the U.S.A.

ISBN-13: 978-1-338-21734-6

SCHOLASTIC and associated logos are trademarks and/or registered trademarks of Scholastic Inc.
Other company names, brand names, and product names are the property and/or trademarks of their respective owners. Scholastic does not endorse any product or business entity mentioned herein.

Contents

Introduction

I'm delighted you have chosen to view *Next Step Guided Reading in Action*. As I travel throughout America, I meet so many people who have purchased my book, *The Next Step in Guided Reading*, and want to know more about guided reading and what it can do for their students. They want to see an actual guided reading lesson and learn for themselves how this approach can transform their reading instruction. Well, I am extremely pleased to present these lessons to you so you can see how I personally plan and teach my guided reading lessons.

An effective guided reading lesson begins with knowing the readers. These videos will show you how I use assessments to determine children's strengths and needs, and how I select a focus for the group. With the focus in mind, I choose the text, plan my introduction, and prompt each student while he or she reads. For me, prompting individual students is the best part of guided reading. Making on-the-spot decisions in a side-by-side conversation with an individual student really takes reading instruction to the next level. I can differentiate my prompting and give each child just enough support to meet the challenges in the text.

To increase the power of guided reading even more, I always include a short guided word-study activity and guided writing. I've repeatedly witnessed how effective these components can be in helping children learn more about phonics and make connections between reading and writing.

I especially hope you will enjoy the narration. We included it so you can know what I was thinking when I planned and taught each lesson. After the lesson is over, I share what my next steps would be for the children in the group.

I love to teach guided reading . . . I hope that comes through loud and clear in this video. My dream is that you, too, will experience the joy of teaching children how to be better readers. Through guided reading, you can help your students establish a strong literacy foundation that will sustain them in school and throughout their lives. Come alongside me as we experience *Next Step Guided Reading in Action*.

THE GUIDED READING STAGES

The following guided reading stages are featured in the videos online (available at Scholastic.com/NSGRActionK2) and in this guide:

- ▶ Pre-A Readers
- ▶ Early Readers
- ▶ Emergent Readers
- ▶ Transitional Readers and Fluent Readers

You can view the video segments sequentially or watch them strategically. For example, if you have emergent and early readers in your classroom, you might concentrate on these segments of the video now, and then watch the next segment on transitional readers as your students progress.

How to Use This Guide

This guide gives you the opportunity to reflect and act upon what you observe in the videos. Each guided reading stage in this guide and on the companion website is divided into four sections:

- ▶ Profile of a reader at that stage
- ▶ A model lesson in action
- ▶ A step-by-step lesson plan
- ▶ Key teaching points

PROFILE This section provides an overview of the skills readers are developing at each stage. You'll also find information on the appropriate texts to use with each stage. After viewing the video, you'll have a chance to think about and assess the readers in your classroom.

LESSON PLAN: STEP BY STEP In the guide, you'll see the framework of a lesson, with management tips about various aspects of guided reading, including group size and the amount of time recommended for each lesson component. After viewing the video, you'll have the tools to group your readers according to their needs and to complete your own lesson plan for a group. Closing out this section is a list of the materials you'll need for your groups, along with management tips or answers to frequently asked questions.

MODEL LESSON IN ACTION This section of the guide shows the completed lesson plan I used to teach the model lesson in the video, including the observations I noted about students' performance. Keep this completed plan handy as you watch me teach the lesson. Additional details about each lesson component appear in the guide. After watching the lesson, you'll use a rubric to evaluate my lesson, and then you'll have a chance to review and refine your own lesson plan. (A printable version of each blank lesson plan is in this guide and also on the website.)

NAVIGATING THROUGH THE MODEL LESSON For the best understanding of how a guided reading lesson works, I recommend watching the Model Lesson videos from start to finish. Should you wish to focus on just one section of the lesson, you can navigate to the Before Reading, Read & Respond, or After Reading sections.

LESSON FRAMEWORK AND THE STANDARDS CHART Each guided reading stage in this guide concludes with a chart aligning lesson objectives with commonly held standards.

REPRODUCIBLES At the end of each stage in this guide, you'll find a template for the lesson plan that you can use to plan your own lessons. An icon in the guide will point you to the forms that appear on the website.

Find your videos & downloadable forms at **scholastic.com/NSGRActionK2**.

ASSESSING YOUR STUDENTS

Assessment is paramount to delivering effective guided reading instruction to your students. Effective assessment should help you answer the following questions:

▶ *How should I group my students?*

▶ *What text should I use with each group?*

▶ *What strategy should I teach?*

In the Profile and Lesson Plan: Step by Step sections described earlier, you'll find assessment guidance and support. I've also recently developed an all-in-one guided reading assessment with my colleague Maria Walther that will give you a complete snapshot of each student. This program will help you determine your students' instructional guided reading range and monitor their progress all year. I think you'll find it takes much less time to administer than some of the more cumbersome assessments you've used.

Next Step Guided Reading Assessment includes a brand-new leveled library complete with literary and informational texts that reflect the complexity recommended by the Common Core State Standards. For more information go to **www.scholastic.com/NextStepGuidedReading**

REFERENCES

Clay, M. (1991). *Becoming literate: The construction of inner control*. Portsmouth, NH: Heinemann.

Davidson, A. (2009). *Playing*. New York: Scholastic.

Dufresne, M. (2006). *A hungry puppy*. Northampton, MA: Pioneer Valley Books.

Dufresne, M. (2010). *Super dog*. Northampton, MA: Pioneer Valley Books.

Dufresne, M. (2011). *Polar bears*. Northampton, MA: Pioneer Valley Books.

Hasbrouck, J., & Tindal, G. A. (2006). ORF norms: A valuable assessment tool for reading teachers. *Reading Teacher, 59*(7), 636–644.

National Governors Association Center for Best Practices & Council of Chief State School Officers. (2010). Common Core State Standards for English Language Arts and Literacy in History/Social Studies, Science, and Technical Subjects. Washington D.C.: National Governors Association Center for Best Practices, Council of Chief State School Officers.

Peters, C. (2009). *Let's play*. New York: Scholastic.

Richardson, J. (2009). *The next step in guided reading: Helping all students become better readers*. New York: Scholastic.

Richardson, J. (2016). *The next step forward in guided reading: An assess-decide-guide framework for supporting every reader*. New York: Scholastic.

Rylant, C. (2001). *The great Gracie chase: Stop that dog!* New York: Scholastic.

Shapiro, S. *Little Red Riding Hood*. San Francisco: Weldon Owen Education, Ltd. Publishing by Scholastic.

Pre-A Readers

The pre-A lesson is designed for nonreaders. They may be kindergartners or students at higher grades who are learning to speak English or have special learning needs. In this section, I'll demonstrate how to:

- ▸ Identify pre-A readers
- ▸ Create a lesson plan for a small group of pre-A readers
- ▸ Teach a pre-A lesson based on the lesson plan
- ▸ Target key teaching points in the lesson

Profile of a Pre-A Reader

Video Running Time: 2:00 | scholastic.com/NSGRActionK2

Take a moment to look at the overview below and then view "Profile of a Pre-Reader."

Who is a pre-A reader? Pre-A readers can identify fewer than 40 upper- and lowercase letters and know few, if any, letter sounds. They probably lack early concepts of print, such as left-to-right tracking and the concept of a letter or word.

Text Reading at the Pre-A Level

Pre-A readers will choral read a very simple Level A guided reading book with mostly known concepts and one line of text per page.

REFLECTION

After you view the video, reflect on the students in your classroom who may be at the pre-A stage. Organize students with similar needs into groups of four or fewer.

ACTION

▶ First, assess your students' knowledge of the alphabet so you can complete the Letter/Sound Checklist. Begin by showing each student an alphabet chart in which the letters are out of sequence. Ask him or her to name the letters. Record both correct and incorrect responses so you can help the child sort out any confusion. To assess sounds, point to a letter and ask the student to tell you the sound it makes. Letter knowledge is directly related to experiences the child has had prior to entering kindergarten. A student who enters kindergarten with strong letter knowledge has been taught the alphabet and possesses good visual memory and discrimination abilities. A meager knowledge of letters does not mean the child has a learning disability. (Form available online)

▶ Use the Class Progress Chart to track the progress of your pre-A readers as they move from one stage to the next. (Form available online)

Reminder

When pre-A students can do the following, they are ready to move to the emergent guided reading lesson:

- Write their first name without a model.

- Identify at least 40 upper- and lowercase letters by name.

- Demonstrate left-to-right directionality across one line of print.

- Understand enough English to follow simple directions.

- Hear a few consonant sounds (at least five).

TEACHING TIP!

TRACE AN ALPHABET BOOK In addition to their guided lessons, pre-A students should trace an alphabet book with a tutor every day. The sooner these children learn the names of the letters, the sooner they will benefit from whole-group and small-group instruction. The tracing process works best if the student's alphabet book has the same pictures as the ones on your classroom alphabet chart or frieze. The goals of the tracing are to teach the name of each letter and to create a picture link for the letter-sound. You can use the Alphabet Chart to make an alphabet book. Enlarge the chart, cut apart the letters and pictures, and staple them in order. (Form available online)

Pre-A Lesson Plan: Step by Step

Video Running Time: 6:16 | scholastic.com/NSGRActionK2

In this video, I explain how to plan and teach a pre-A lesson. Before you view the video, take a moment to look at the Pre-A Lesson Framework chart below.

What does the pre-A lesson framework look like? Pre-A students who need nascent literacy skills learn a great deal from whole-group activities such as read-alouds, shared reading, and interactive writing. Their specific needs, however, are best addressed in small groups with the pre-A lesson plan. A pre-A lesson has four distinct components designed to improve visual memory, letter knowledge, phonemic awareness, oral language, and concepts of print. The chart below shows the components of the pre-A lesson and their corresponding target skills. It also tells how long to spend on each component.

Pre-A Lesson Framework	
Lesson Component	**Target Skills**
Before Reading **Working With Letters and Names** *(3–4 minutes)*	• Visual memory (with children's own names) • Letter names • Visual discrimination • Visual scanning (left to right across a word)
Working With Sounds *(2–3 minutes)*	• Phonological awareness (hearing syllables and rhymes) • Phonemic awareness (hearing initial consonants) • Auditory discrimination (hearing the difference between sounds)
Read & Respond **Working With Books** *(5 minutes)*	• Concepts of print (left-to-right tracking, one-to-one matching, concept of letter/word, first/last, capital/lowercase) • Oral language and English syntax • Vocabulary (picture concepts)
After Reading **Interactive Writing** *(5 minutes)*	• Phonemic awareness (hearing consonant sounds) • Linking consonant sounds to letters • Letter formation • Concepts of print (left-to-right tracking, spacing between words, capital/lowercase letters, concept of letter/word, and first/last)

For an in-depth explanation of the procedures for a pre-A lesson, see Description of the Pre-A Lesson Plan on pages 62–71 of *The Next Step in Guided Reading* (pages 35–47 of *The Next Step Forward in Guided Reading*).

TIME FRAME FOR A PRE-A LESSON Allot 15–20 minutes for a lesson. Include one activity from each lesson component. Using a timer and limiting teacher talk will help you transition between activities every few minutes. It will also keep your students engaged and focused. At the beginning of the year, some students may have difficulty sitting at a table for 20 minutes. If necessary, teach the lesson in two parts. Do the first two components for about 10 minutes and then later in the day or on the following day, teach the last two components of the lesson.

PRE-A GROUP SIZE: NO MORE THAN FOUR Group students according to their letter knowledge, but do not put more than four students in a group. For example, place the four children who know the fewest letters in the same group so you can better target their needs.

REFLECTION

View "Pre-A Lesson Plan: Step by Step" and then reflect on the needs of the students in your classroom. Think about how you will group your students. Decide which letters and sounds you should teach each group.

ACTION

▶ Complete an Assessment Summary Chart for Pre-A and Emergent Readers A–C. (Form available online)

▶ Prepare a Letter/Sound Checklist for each pre-A group by highlighting each student's known letters and sounds. Use the data on the group's Letter/Sound Checklist to determine which letters and sounds to teach. Reassess your pre-A students on their letter knowledge at least once a month and update the group checklist when a student has learned a new letter or sound. (Form available online)

▶ Use your completed Assessment Summary Chart and your completed Letter/Sound Checklist to ensure that your groupings meet your students' needs.

Reminder: Using the Letter/Sound Checklist

Have this checklist handy as you teach a lesson. Circle or highlight new letters students are beginning to recognize. Expect inconsistency with these letters. It will likely take several lessons before the new letter knowledge becomes firm. This information will inform your future lesson plans.

▶ Now it's time to fill out your own lesson plan. Use the Pre-A Lesson Plan on page 17 to design a lesson for one group that you've targeted.

▶ Review my explanation of each lesson component on the video as you work. Additional information appears on the next page.

① EIGHT WAYS OF WORKING WITH LETTERS

LETTER ACTIVITY Make a personal letter bag of known letters for each student (see the materials list on page 12). If a student knows fewer than 10 letters, include duplicates of each known letter and the letters in the student's name. Students will use the bags to do one letter activity (see Eight Ways of Working With Letters on the website).

LETTER FORMATION Select a letter that most students in the group know by name.

② WORKING WITH NAMES

Choose one activity. Name puzzles and making the name out of magnetic letters are the easiest. Rainbow writing is more challenging because it requires that students actually write their names. *Note: This component can be omitted once children know the letters in their first name and can write their first name with correct letter formation.*

③ WORKING WITH SOUNDS

Choose one activity. Most students learn to clap syllables and hear rhymes before they can isolate beginning sounds. For picture sorts, select two sounds that most students need to learn.

④ WORKING WITH BOOKS

Select a very simple, Level A guided reading book. It should have one line of print per page and mostly familiar concepts. Do not use big books. Children are more engaged when they can hold a text in their hands. Before reading, guide students through the book and encourage conversations about the pictures. This will strengthen their oral language. Then have students read the book with you while they point to each word with a pointer. After reading, select one or two teaching points. Refer to page 15 for target skills.

⑤ INTERACTIVE WRITING

Dictate a simple sentence of four to six words that is related to the book the group has just read. Try to include the sounds students sorted during the Working With Sounds components.

Pre-A Lesson Plan

Student: _____ Date: _____ Lesson#: _____

Activity Options	Observations/Notes
Eight Ways of Working With Letters	
① Letter Activity: #_____ Letter Formation: _____	
Working With Names (Choose 1) ② ❏ Use name puzzles. ❏ Make names out of magnetic letters. ❏ Do rainbow writing with names.	
Working With Sounds (Choose 1) ③ Clapping syllables 1 2 3 Rhyming words _____ Picture sorts _____	
Working With Books Do shared reading with a level A book. Encourage oral language and teach print concepts (choose one or two): ④ ❏ Concept of a word (students frame each word in a sentence) ❏ First/last word (students locate in text) ❏ Concept of a letter (students frame a letter or count the letters in a word) ❏ First/last letter (students locate in text) ❏ Period (students locate in text) ❏ Capital/lowercase letters (students locate in text)	Title: _____ Observations: _____ _____ _____ _____ _____
Interactive Writing & Cut-Up Sentence ⑤ Sentence:	

Materials You Will Need for the Pre-A Lesson

For each group, gather the following materials:

- Alphabet Chart (1 for each student): Place a copy of the Alphabet Chart inside a clear, heavy sheet protector. (Form available online)

- Name template for rainbow writing: Print each child's first name on a sheet of paper. Place this template inside the sheet protector that holds the Alphabet Chart so the template appears on one side and the chart on the other.

- Personal letter bag: Label a quart-size plastic bag with each student's name and fill it with magnetic letters that the student knows and the letters in the student's first name. If he or she knows fewer than 10 letters, include duplicates of each letter (lowercase or both upper- and lowercase forms). Once the student knows 10 letters, remove the duplicates and place only lowercase letters in the bag. As students learn new letters, add them to the bag.

- Dry-erase markers and eraser (1 for you and for each student)

- Wooden craft sticks or plastic straws to use as pointers (1 for each student)

- Pictures for initial consonant sorts

- Sentence strips and scissors

- Easy Level A books with one line of text per page

- Pre-A Lesson Plan (several copies): A reproducible appears on page 17.

- Timer

MANAGEMENT TIPS! During the first six weeks of school, establish routines for your reading workshop. Students must learn how to work in teams, how to solve problems without asking for your help, and how to use workstations or do other independent literacy activities.

▶ Decide where you will teach the groups. If you don't already have a small-group area in your classroom, procure a table where you and up to four students can sit. Situate the table so you will be able to keep an eye on the entire classroom. Organize your materials on a nearby bookshelf or rolling cart positioned next to you.

▶ Decide when you will teach the groups. Analyze your schedule and set priorities. You may decide to alternate your small-group and whole-group instruction so you can gather students together after 20 minutes of literacy centers to reinforce appropriate, independent behaviors.

▶ Decide what your other students will be doing while you're teaching the groups. While you work with small groups, the other students should be involved in literacy-related activities. Literacy centers or workstations provide opportunities for them to engage in purposeful learning activities.

Here are some easy workstation activities: Book Boxes for independent reading, Buddy Reading, Big Books, Read the Room (or Word Hunt), Writing, Listening, Poems and Songs, ABC/Word Study, Computer, Oral Retelling of books you have read to the class, and Library.

Model Lesson in Action: Pre-A Reader

Video Running Time: 15:39 | scholastic.com/NSGRActionK2

In this video, I demonstrate a pre-A lesson with a group of four students, three of whom are learning English as a second language. I chose the book *Playing* by Avelyn Davidson because students are familiar with the concepts, it has pictures that reinforce the text, and the spaces between the words aid in one-to-one matching.

Take a moment to look at the completed lesson plan with my observations below and then view the video. I suggest you download and print the completed Pre-A Lesson Plan and refer to it as you watch the lesson.

Pre-A Lesson Plan

Student: Emily, Cindy, Cinthia, Douglas   Date: _____   Lesson# _____

Activity Options	Observations/Notes
Before Reading	
Eight Ways of Working With Letters Letter Activity: # 8 Letter Formation: K	Letter/Sound Knowledge |	m	t	j	f	K
---	---	---	---	---	---
Emily	✓	✓	✓		
Cindy					
Cinthia	✓	✓	✓	✓	
Douglas	✓				✓	
Working With Names (Choose 1) ☐ Use name puzzles. ☐ Make names out of magnetic letters. ☐ Do rainbow writing with names.	"Start at top" - prompt K need a little support with formation
Working With Sounds (Choose 1) Clapping syllables 1 2 3 Rhyming words _____ Picture sorts l-r	needed support making the "l" + "r" sounds. Able to link to letter when I said the sound.
Read & Respond	
Working With Books Do shared reading with a level A book. Encourage oral language and teach print concepts (choose one or two): ☒ Concept of a word (students frame each word in a sentence) ☐ First/last word (students locate in text) ☐ Concept of a letter (students frame a letter or count the letters in a word) ☐ First/last letter (students locate in text) ☐ Period (students locate in text) ☐ Capital/lowercase letters (students locate in text)	Title: Playing -discuss pictures Observations: ✱ Strengths: 1:1, used pictures Teaching point - used finger framing to identify a word.
After Reading	
Interactive Writing & Cut-Up Sentence Sentence: We like to run.	Strengths: heard sounds, linked sounds to letters, good formation. Able to remake sentence using beginning sound.

✱✱ Ready for Emergent Guided Reading ✱✱

As you watch the video, notice how I quickly transition from one activity to the next to keep children engaged. Notice, too, that I have all my materials organized and ready to use.

BEFORE READING

EIGHT WAYS OF WORKING WITH LETTERS The Letter Activity I selected was "Find the letter that makes that sound." These pre-A students are progressing, but they still need practice in matching sounds and letters. The eight activities listed in the video appear from easiest to hardest. The first is geared toward students who know very few letters, while activities 6, 7, and 8 are designed for students who know 30 or more letters by name.

Notice that the last letter students find in the Letter Activity is *K*, which is the same letter they work on in Letter Formation. Writing the letter *K* will give them practice in writing letters that have slanted lines.

WORKING WITH NAMES Since these students can write their names without a model and know all the letters in their names, I haven't included an activity for this component.

WORKING WITH SOUNDS In the picture sorts for *l* and *r*, I say the names of the pictures on the cards as I distribute them to students. Since some of these children are English language learners, they are probably not familiar with all the picture concepts. They know *l* and *r* by name, but sometimes they confuse the sounds of the letters.

READ & RESPOND

WORKING WITH BOOKS Although this group of students demonstrates one-to-one matching, they still don't understand the concept of a word, so that becomes my teaching point. The book *Playing* has good spacing between words and that allows students to easily frame each word.

Because there are three ELLs in this group, it is especially important for me to present a strong oral introduction. As part of the introduction, I ask them to take turns looking at a picture and explaining what it shows. Then I model a patterned sentence that matches the picture, and I ask students to repeat the sentence with me.

CONCEPT OF A WORD ACTIVITY In this lesson, I encourage students to frame each word with their fingers. Another activity that helps children understand the concept of a word is to have them count the words during the Interactive Writing component.

After Reading

INTERACTIVE WRITING & CUT-UP SENTENCE For this activity, I took a sentence directly from the text, "We like to run." I chose this sentence because it includes *like* and *run*, which begin with *l* and *r*, the letters we worked on during the picture sorts. The sentence also gave students an opportunity to practice forming the letter *k*, which was the letter I taught at the beginning of the lesson. You don't have to use a sentence from the book. The important thing is to include the sounds and letters you teach during the lesson so children have the opportunity to apply these skills during writing. Creating the sentence yourself instead of letting children help you will save time and keep them focused. Notice how students take turns writing the dominant consonant sounds in each word, and I write the sounds they don't know. The words in the sentence should be spelled correctly. Since this is interactive writing, I don't allow invented spelling. This is also a good opportunity to teach correct letter formation.

Target Skills and Strategies

For more information on the following skills and strategies, see the "Teaching Points" video clips:

- Describe in Complete Sentences: Encourage students to describe the picture using a complete sentence.

- Use One-to-One Matching: Each child should use a small pointer to point to the words as he or she reads each page.

- Check the Picture to Decode the Word: This is an important emergent reading strategy that supports the development of comprehension.

- Understand the Concept of a Word: Students often confuse the concept of *letter* and *word*. Have them frame each word on a page or two in the book.

- Match Sounds to Letters: If students need help linking sounds and letters, direct them to pictures on the Alphabet Chart.

Reflection

Take time to review my model lesson. Based on what you saw, would you make any changes in your lesson plans?

Action

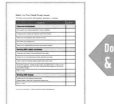

▶ Complete the Rubric for "Pre-A Small Group Lesson" to evaluate its components. Review the video as necessary to help you fill in the rubric. (Form available online)

▶ Review and refine your lesson plan.

▶ Teach your lesson. Remember to use the notes and observations you made on your lesson plan and the Letter/Sound Checklist to assess your students' performance and progress.

THE PRE-A LESSON FRAMEWORK: ADDRESSING STANDARDS

The chart below shows how each component of the Pre-A Lesson Framework aligns with commonly held state and national standards.

Pre-A Lesson Component/ Objective	Standards*
Working With Letters and Names • Name letters • Letter/ sound links	**FOUNDATIONAL** **Print Concepts: K.1.d** Recognize and name all upper- and lowercase letters of the alphabet. **Phonics and Word Recognition: K.3.a** Demonstrate basic knowledge of one-to-one letter-sound correspondences by producing the primary sound or many of the most frequent sounds for each consonant.
Working With Sounds • Rhymes • Syllables • Initial sounds	**FOUNDATIONAL** **Phonological Awareness: K.2.a** Recognize and produce rhyming words. **K.2.b** Count, pronounce, blend, and segment syllables in spoken words. **K.2.d** Isolate and pronounce the initial, medial vowel, and final sounds (phonemes) in three-phoneme (CVC) words. **Phonics and Word Recognition: K.3.a** Demonstrate basic knowledge of one-to-one letter-sound correspondences by producing the primary sound or many of the most frequent sounds for each consonant.
Working With Books • Print concepts • Oral language	**FOUNDATIONAL** **Print Concepts: K.1.a** Follow words from left to right, top to bottom, and page by page. **K.1.b** Recognize that spoken words are represented in written language by specific sequences of letters. **K.1.c** Understand that words are separated by spaces in print. **LANGUAGE** **Grammar and Usage: K.1.b** Use frequently occurring nouns and verbs. **K.1.c** Form regular plural nouns orally by adding /s/ or /es/. **K.1.d** Understand and use question words. **K.1.e** Use the most frequently occurring prepositions. **K.1.f** Produce and expand complete sentences in shared language activities.
Interactive Writing Hear and record sounds, conventions, language	**LANGUAGE** **Grammar and Usage: K.1.a** Print many upper- and lowercase letters. **Capitalization, Punctuation, and Spelling: K.2.a** Capitalize the first word in a sentence and the pronoun *I*. **K.2.b** Recognize and name end punctuation. **K.2.c** Write a letter or letters for most consonant and short-vowel sounds (phonemes). **K.2.d** Spell simple words phonetically, drawing on knowledge of sound-letter relationships.

*The Common Core State Standards are used here as a point of reference.

Pre-A Lesson Plan

Student: _____ Date: _____ Lesson#: _____

Activity Options	Observations/Notes
Eight Ways of Working With Letters Letter Activity: #_____ Letter Formation: _____	
Working With Names (Choose 1) ❑ Use name puzzles. ❑ Make names out of magnetic letters. ❑ Do rainbow writing with names.	
Working With Sounds (Choose 1) Clapping syllables 1 2 3 Rhyming words _____ Picture sorts _____	
Working With Books Do shared reading with a level A book. Encourage oral language and teach print concepts (choose one or two): ❑ Concept of a word (students frame each word in a sentence) ❑ First/last word (students locate in text) ❑ Concept of a letter (students frame a letter or count the letters in a word) ❑ First/last letter (students locate in text) ❑ Period (students locate in text) ❑ Capital/lowercase letters (students locate in text)	Title: _____ Observations: _____ _____ _____ _____ _____
Interactive Writing & Cut-Up Sentence Sentence:	

TM ® & © Scholastic Inc. All rights reserved. *The Next Step in Guided Reading* copyright © 2009 by Jan Richardson. Published by Scholastic Inc.

Emergent Readers

The emergent guided reading lesson is designed for kindergarten and first-grade students who are just beginning to read; it is also for children at higher grade levels who are learning to speak English or have a special need for emergent skills and strategies. In this section, I'll demonstrate how to:

▶ Identify emergent readers
▶ Create a lesson plan for a small group of emergent readers
▶ Teach an emergent lesson based on the lesson plan
▶ Target key teaching points in the lesson

Profile of an Emergent Reader

Video Running Time: 1:59 | *scholastic.com/NSGRActionK2*

Take a moment to look at the overview below and then view "Profile of an Emergent Reader."

Who is an emergent reader? Emergent readers can write their first names without a model, identify at least 40 upper- and lowercase letters by name, demonstrate left-to-right directionality, understand enough English to follow simple directions, and hear at least five consonant sounds.

Text Reading at the Emergent Level

Emergent readers will read Levels A–C guided reading books. At the beginning of this stage, focus on repetitive patterned books to help students learn high-frequency words, but choose less patterned texts as readers move to the higher end of the emergent stage. This shift will require children to use more visual cues to problem-solve new words.

REFLECTION

After you view the video, think about students in your classroom who may be at the emergent stage. Organize them into groups that have similar needs and are not more than one reading level apart. For example, you might put some students at levels A and B together because they know many letters but very few sight words. You might also be able to place B and C students together because they hear sounds in words but are not using them during reading to cross-check.

ACTION

The chart shows several different types of assessments you can use to form emergent guided reading groups.

Assessment	Information
Dictated sentence	• Phonemic awareness: ability to hear sounds in words, link sounds to letters, and write the sounds in sequence • Letter formation • Concepts of print: left-to-right directionality, spacing, return sweep, punctuation • Spelling of high-frequency words
Writing sample	• Language skills: English syntax, vocabulary, ability to construct an idea • Phonemic awareness/phonics skills: hearing sounds in sequence, sound/letter links, spelling of high-frequency words, letter formation • Concepts of print: directionality, spacing, return sweep, punctuation
Word list	• Sight-word knowledge, decoding skills
Running record	• Strategies, reading levels

▶ Complete the Assessment Summary Chart to organize your assessment information and to help you form groups according to students' needs. For more information on how to fill in the chart, see "Directions for Using the Assessment Summary for Emergent Readers." (Forms available online)

▶ Utilize the Class Progress Chart to track the progress of your emergent readers throughout the year. (Form available online)

Emergent Guided Reading Lesson Plan: Step by Step

Video Running Time: 8:22 | *scholastic.com/NSGRActionK2*

In this video, I explain how to plan and teach an emergent lesson. Before you view the video, take a moment to look at the Emergent Lesson Framework below.

What does the emergent lesson framework look like? Each emergent guided reading lesson focuses on teaching appropriate skills and strategies.

Emergent Reading Skills	Emergent Reading Strategies
• Form letters • Know all letters and sounds • Hear sounds in sequence (consonant-vowel-consonant) • Put spaces between words during writing	• Employ one-to-one matching • Use meaning (picture clues) and initial letters to figure out unknown words • Segment sounds to write unknown words • Use meaning, known words, and initial letters to self-monitor during reading and writing • Discuss a story with teacher prompting

The chart below shows the components of a two-day emergent guided reading lesson like the one I teach in the video.

Emergent Lesson Framework	
DAY 1: Lesson Component	**DAY 2: Lesson Component**
Before Reading Sight Word Review—Writing *(1–2 min)*	Sight Word Review—Writing *(1–2 min)*
Introduce New Book: Title/Gist New Vocabulary *(3–4 min)*	Rereading of Yesterday's Book (and other familiar books) while teacher prompts individual students *(5–8 min)*
Read & Respond Text Reading With Prompting *(5–8 min)*	
Teaching Points After Reading *(1–2 min)*	Teaching Points After Reading *(1–2 min)*
Discussion Prompt	Discussion Prompt
After Reading Teach One Sight Word *(1–2 min)*	Teach Same Sight Word *(1 min)*
Word Study *(3–5 min)*	Guided Writing *(8–10 min)*

For an in-depth explanation of the procedures for an emergent guided reading lesson, see Description of the Emergent Guided Reading Lesson (Two-Day Plan) on pages 86–95 of *The Next Step in Guided Reading* (pages 68–94 of *The Next Step Forward in Guided Reading*).

TEACHING AN INDIVIDUAL EMERGENT READER There are occasions when you may want to do an individual guided reading lesson because a particular student does not fit into any group. This is often a short-term problem since groupings change frequently. A three-day lesson plan designed for individuals, and procedures for teaching it, are on the website.

TIME FRAME FOR AN EMERGENT GUIDED READING LESSON Allot 15–20 minutes for a lesson. Using a timer and limiting teacher talk will help you transition between activities every few minutes—and keep your students engaged and focused.

EMERGENT GROUP SIZE: UP TO SIX The video shows groups of three and four, but your emergent guided groups can have up to six students. Continue to update your Assessment Summary Chart monthly and use the information to regroup students for guided reading.

REFLECTION

View "Emergent Guided Reading Lesson Plan: Step by Step" and then reflect on the needs of the students in your classroom. Consider how you'll group them. Then, think about the lesson plan:

▶ *Which sight words will you review?*

▶ *Which book would offer enough challenge and success for this group? Does it contain mostly known sight words and one sight word you could teach?*

▶ *Which phonics skills are students ready to learn during the word study portion?*

▶ *What dictated sentence would be appropriate for guided writing?*

CROSS-CHECKING Always teach the cross-checking strategy to children reading level A or B books. To encourage cross-checking behavior, give students choices when you discuss the pictures during the introduction. For example, you could say, "It might be a horse or a pony. You'll have to check the first letter when you read to figure it out."

ACTION

▶ Complete an Assessment Summary Chart for Pre-A and Emergent Readers A–C. (Form available online)

▶ Use your completed Assessment Summary Chart to ensure that your groupings meet your students' needs. If students haven't yet mastered all the letters of the alphabet, teach those letters and sounds during the word study and monitor students' progress on a Letter/Sound Checklist. (Form available online)

▶ Now it's time to fill out your own lesson plan. Use the Emergent Guided Reading Lesson Plan on page 31 to design a plan for one of your emergent groups.

▶ Review my explanation of each lesson component in the video as you work. Additional information appears on the next page.

① SIGHT WORD REVIEW—WRITING

Refer to the High-Frequency Word Chart to select three sight words you have previously taught. Ideally, choose sight words that appear in the new book. (Form available online)

② INTRODUCE NEW BOOK

Guide students as they discuss the pictures and make predictions. Support students' oral language, if necessary, and teach any new vocabulary.

③ TEXT READING WITH PROMPTING

On Day 1, students read the book independently with prompting from you. On Day 2, students reread the book and other familiar books.

④ TEACHING POINTS AFTER READING

Select cross-checking and one or more teaching points based on your assessment of the group's needs.

⑤ DISCUSSION PROMPT

If the text is complex enough, ask a question to explore comprehension.

⑥ TEACH ONE SIGHT WORD/ TEACH SAME SIGHT WORD

On Day 1, introduce a new sight word. Again, use the High-Frequency Word Chart on the website to make your selection. Use all four activities in sequence to teach the word. On Day 2, review the word using all four activities again.

⑦ WORD STUDY

On Day 1, choose one of the options that is listed on the lesson plan.

⑧ GUIDED WRITING

On Day 2, use a dictated or an open-ended sentence that includes some of the known sight words and the new sight word.

Reminder

When emergent readers have mastered the following skills, they are ready to move to the early guided reading lesson:

- Consistently demonstrate one-to-one matching
- Use meaning (picture clues) and initial letters to figure out unknown words
- Segment sounds to write unknown words
- Use meaning, known words, and initial letters to self-monitor during reading and writing
- Discuss a story with teacher prompting

Materials You Will Need for the Emergent Lesson

For each group, gather the following materials:

- Alphabet Chart (1 for each student): Place the Alphabet Chart inside a clear, heavy sheet protector. (Form available online)

- Letter/Sound Checklist (if students do not know all of their letters and sounds) (Form available online)

- Dry-erase boards, markers, and erasers (1 for each student)

- Sets of lowercase magnetic letters (6–8 sets)

- Pictures for sound sorts (initial consonants and short medial vowels)

- Blank journal (1 for each student)

- Assessment kit, which includes leveled reading passages, comprehension questions, and a word knowledge inventory

- Leveled books (A–C)

- Emergent Guided Reading Lesson Plan (several copies): A reproducible appears on page 31.

- High-Frequency Word Chart (1 for each group): Record the high-frequency words students can write on the chart. I do not keep track of the words students are able to read in isolation. If children know how to write a word, they can usually read that word. Use the information on this chart to select guided reading books, plan your word study, and create your dictated sentences for guided writing. (Form available online)

- Sound Box Template (place in a heavy plastic sheet protector): Students will use this template for segmenting words during word study. (Form available online)

- Timer

SOME COMMONLY ASKED QUESTIONS

What assessments should I use? As long as you have a leveled text, you can find the instructional level with a running record and an oral retell. If you prefer a commercial assessment package, select one with short, leveled passages and a comprehension component, such as *Next Step Guided Reading Assessment* (see page 6). When assessing emergent readers, use passages or books with pictures.

Why should I take a running record? Running records capture the reading process of emergent, early, and transitional readers. An analysis of the errors reveals the strategies a child uses when he or she is having difficulty and the strategies the child needs to learn next. For more information, visit scholastic.com/NextStepGuidedReading.

Why do you teach the new sight word after the reading of the book and not before? Students have had the opportunity to see the word in context. Use *What's Missing?, Mix & Fix, Table Writing,* and *Writing on a Whiteboard* to teach the word in depth. On Day 1, before students read the book, write the word on the whiteboard or simply say it and have students find it in the book.

Model Lesson in Action: Emergent Reader

Video Running Time: 18:55 | *scholastic.com/NSGRActionK2*

In this video, I show what an emergent lesson looks and sounds like with a group of three ELL kindergartners. I chose the book *Let's Play* by Catherine Peters because the pictures help students understand the new vocabulary, and it contains some known sight words.

Take a moment to look at the completed lesson plan with my observations below and then view the video. I suggest you download and print the completed Emergent Guided Reading Lesson Plan and refer to it as you watch the lesson.

Emergent Guided Reading Lesson Plan

Title: __Let's Play__   Level: __A/B__   Lesson #: _____

	Day 1 Date: _____	**Day 2** Date: _____
Before Reading	**Sight Word Review—Writing** to _____ We _____ on _____	**Sight Word Review—Writing** like _____ the _____ go _____
	Introduce New Book: This book is called __Let's Play__ and it's about __two children who like to pretend they are playing. Have you ever pretended you were playing something?__ **New vocabulary:** __plane, hill, ship, love__	**Rereading of Yesterday's Book (and other familiar books)** Observations: —Children did well with cross-checking. Checked picture and got their mouths ready to problem-solve. —Often miscued on sight words. They need to monitor with known words as they read. —Need to firm up short vowel sounds. Do more picture sorts. — Able to generate their own sentences.
Read & Respond	**Text Reading With Prompting:** ☒ Check the picture. What would make sense? ☒ Get your mouth ready for the first sound. ☐ Get your mouth ready and check the picture. ☐ Could it be _____ or _____? ☒ Show me the word _____ ☐ Check the word with your finger. Are you right? ☐ Try reading without pointing. ☐ How would the character say that? (show expression)	
	Teaching Points After Reading (choose one or two each day): ☐ One-to-one matching (at level C, discourage pointing) ☐ Use picture clues (meaning) ☐ Monitor with known words ☐ Get mouth ready for initial sound ☒ Cross-check picture and first letter ☐ Visual scanning (check the word left to right) ☐ Fluency and expression	
	Discussion Prompt (if appropriate): What did they pretend they were playing on?	**Discussion Prompt (if appropriate):** Why do they like to pretend?
After Reading	**Teach One Sight Word:** __like__ • What's missing? • Table Writing • Mix & Fix • Writing on a whiteboard	**Teach Same Sight Word:** __like__ • What's missing? • Table Writing • Mix & Fix • Writing on a whiteboard
	Word Study (Choose just one): ☐ Picture sorts: _____ ☐ Making words: _____ ☒ Sound boxes: __Sat, hop, bag__	**Guided Writing:** Dictated or open-ended sentence We like to go on the rocks. Students generate second sentence. NOTE: Independently stretched out words. Good phonetic spelling on rocks.

Day 1

BEFORE READING

SIGHT WORD REVIEW—WRITING For the sight word review, I often choose words in the new book that I have taught in previous lessons. That way I am reinforcing the known words that students can use to monitor their reading.

INTRODUCE NEW BOOK AND VOCABULARY

Main Idea Statement: State the title of the book and give a simple "gist" statement.

Story Walk: Do a story walk of the book and invite students to talk about the pictures and make predictions. Encourage those who have limited English to say a complete sentence in response to a prompt; for example, "Tell me who is in the picture and what they are doing." Model a complete sentence if necessary.

Sight Word: Introduce the new sight word by having students predict the first letter and locate the word in the text. Do not write the word on the whiteboard or create it out of magnetic letters now; this happens after reading.

Concepts: Discuss any unfamiliar concepts in the text.

Cross-checking: To encourage cross-checking behavior, give students choices when you come across pictures of familiar concepts. You do not need to write the words on the whiteboard or have students locate them in the text. You are building background with the words so students can search meaning and visual cues when they see them in the book.

READ & RESPOND

TEXT READING WITH PROMPTING Students read the book independently with your prompting. If you notice two students reading the same page, ask one to go back a page and read it to you. The goal of this component is not accurate reading but active processing. Listen to individual students and prompt for strategic behaviors when someone stops or makes an error. Even if a student makes no errors, it is still important to prompt for emergent strategies. Take notes about each student's performance on the back of your lesson plan.

TEACHING POINTS AFTER READING Use your notes to choose one or two teaching points. At Levels A–B, always do the cross-checking teaching point. This is where you select a few random pages from the story, cover the picture, and have students chorally read while you point to the words. Encourage children to sound the first letter when they come to an unknown word. Then show them the picture. They should be able to cross-check the picture and the first letter without your prompting before you move them to the next level.

Target Skills and Strategies

For more information on the following skills and strategies, see the "Teaching Points" video clips:

- **Match Sounds to Letters:** Saying a word as they write it helps students match the sound they hear to the letter they write.
- **Cross-Check Initial Letter With Picture:** Students cross-check by using picture clues and the first letter of a word to figure out the word's meaning.
- **Use One-to-One Matching:** Have students use pointers until they have a strong grasp of one-to-one matching.
- **Read With Fluency:** When students master one-to-one matching, discontinue the use of pointers to develop fluency.
- **Build Automaticity With Sight Words:** When students quickly point out words, even those that can't be easily decoded, they are building automaticity.

DISCUSSION PROMPT The question I asked on Day 1, "What did they (the children in the story) like to pretend to play on?" helped students recall what they read.

AFTER READING

TEACH ONE SIGHT WORD You will teach the same sight word for at least two days. The purpose of this component is to help students develop visual memory and increase their bank of high-frequency words. Follow the procedures on the lesson plan each day with every word in this sequence: *What's Missing?*, *Mix & Fix*, *Table Writing*, and *Writing on a Whiteboard*. These four steps gradually release the responsibility for writing the word from the teacher to the student. Review the video to see how I incorporate each procedure into the lesson. You may need to work on the same sight word for more than two days. Don't introduce a new word until students can write the previous one without support.

WORD STUDY Choose one of these three options, listed from easiest to hardest: *picture sorts*, *making words*, or *sound boxes*. Teach these specific skills at each level:

- ▶ Level A: hearing initial consonants

- ▶ Level B: hearing final consonants and medial short vowels (*a* and *o*)

- ▶ Level C: hearing medial short vowels (*i*, *e*, and *u*) and recording CVC words in sequence

In the video, you'll notice that I have students use Sound Boxes to work on Level B skills, short-*a* and short-*o*.

Reminder

In this video, I teach a complete Day 1 lesson and the Guided Writing portion from Day 2.

Day 2

BEFORE READING

SIGHT WORD REVIEW—WRITING Follow the same procedures for Day 1, but use three different sight words that students already know. One of the review words should be the new sight word you introduced in Day 1.

READ & RESPOND

REREADING OF YESTERDAY'S BOOK (AND OTHER FAMILIAR BOOKS)
If students are able to read the Day 1 book quickly several times, give them other familiar books they have read in previous guided reading lessons.

TEACHING POINTS AFTER READING Choose one or two teaching points based on the group's needs; use the same procedure as in Day 1.

DISCUSSION PROMPT If the text can support it, ask a question that explores deeper comprehension.

AFTER READING

TEACH SAME SIGHT WORD Teach the same sight word you taught on Day 1. Be sure to follow these four procedures in sequence: *What's Missing?*, *Mix & Fix*, *Table Writing*, and *Writing on a Whiteboard.*

GUIDED WRITING In the model lesson, I created a sentence that contained familiar sight words, the new sight word, and an unknown word (*rocks*) they could sound out—*We like to go on the rocks.* Then, I encouraged children to create their own sentences using the stem *We like to go on the _____.* To help them put spaces between the words, I drew a blank for each word in the sentence in their writing journals. Once students are able to space words without prompting, you can discontinue drawing the lines.

BLANK WRITING JOURNAL Make a writing journal for each student by folding about 15 sheets of paper in half and stapling. Have students write in these journals rather than on the whiteboards so you have a record of their attempts and successes. Use the top part of the journal for practicing a sight word or demonstrating correct letter formation.

TEACHING TIP!

CORRECT SPELLING FOR SIGHT WORDS Sight words you have taught must be spelled correctly. If a student misspells a sight word, write the correct spelling on the top page of their writing journal and have them practice writing it. You can accept invented spelling for unknown words; this will encourage children to take risks. Be sure they say the word slowly and write the sounds they hear.

Reflection

Take time to evaluate my model lesson. Based on what you saw, would you make any changes in your lesson plan?

Action

▶ Complete the Rubric for Emergent Guided Reading Lesson (Levels A–C) to evaluate its components. Review the video as necessary to help you fill in the rubric.

▶ Review and refine your lesson plan.

▶ Teach your lesson. Remember to use the notes and observations on your lesson plan (and the Letter/Sound Checklist, if applicable) to assess your students' performance and progress.

The Emergent Guided Reading Lesson Framework: Addressing Standards

The chart below shows how each component of the Emergent Lesson Framework aligns with commonly held state and national standards.

Emergent Lesson Component/ Objective	Standards*
Sight Word Review—Writing • High-frequency words	**FOUNDATIONAL** **Phonics and Word Recognition: K.3**, **1.3** Know and apply grade-level phonics and word analysis skills in decoding words. **LANGUAGE** **Conventions: K.2.d** Spell simple words phonetically, drawing on sound-letter relationships.
Introduce New Book • Oral language • Print concepts	**LITERATURE** **Integration of Knowledge and Ideas: K.7** With prompting and support, describe the relationship between illustrations and the story in which they appear. **1.7** Use illustrations and details in a story to describe its characters, setting, or events.

LITERATURE

Key Ideas and Details: K.1 With prompting and support, ask and answer questions about key details in a text. **K.3** With prompting and support, identify characters, settings, and major events in a story. **1.1** Ask and answer questions about key details in a text. **1.3** Describe characters, settings, and major events in a story, using details. **Craft and Structure: 1.6** Identify who is telling the story at various points in a text. **Integration of Knowledge and Ideas K.7** With prompting and support, describe the relationship between illustrations and the story in which they appear. **1.7** Use illustrations and details in a story to describe its characters, setting, or events. **Range of Reading and Level of Text Complexity: K.10** Actively engage in group reading activities with purpose and understanding. **1.10** With prompting and support, read prose of appropriate complexity for grade 1.

Reading With Text Prompting

- Oral language
- Print concepts

INFORMATIONAL TEXT

Key Ideas and Details: K.1 With prompting and support, ask and answer questions about key details in a text. **K.3** With prompting and support, describe the connection between two individuals, events, ideas, or pieces of information in a text. **1.1** Ask and answer questions about key details in a text. **1.3** Describe the connection between two individuals, events, ideas, or pieces of information in a text. **Craft and Structure: 1.6** Distinguish between information provided by pictures or other illustrations and information provided by other words in text. **Integration of Knowledge and Ideas: K.7** With prompting and support, describe the relationship between illustrations and the text in which they appear. **1.7** Use illustrations and details in a story to describe its key ideas. **Range of Reading and Level of Text Complexity: K.10** Actively engage in group reading activities with purpose and understanding. **1.10** With prompting and support, read informational texts appropriately complex for grade 1.

FOUNDATIONAL

Print Concepts: K.1, **1.1** Demonstrate understanding of the organization and basic features of print. **Fluency: K.4** Read emergent-reader texts with purpose and understanding. **1.4** Read with sufficient accuracy and fluency to support comprehension.

Teaching Points After Reading • Strategies and skills	**READING LITERATURE** **Key Ideas and Details: K.1** With prompting and support, ask and answer questions about key details in a text. **K.3** With prompting and support, identify characters, settings, and major events in a story. **1.1** Ask and answer questions about key details in a text.**1.3** Describe characters, settings, and major events in a story, using details. **Craft and Structure: 1.6** Identify who is telling the story at various points in a text. **Integration of Knowledge and Ideas: K.7** With prompting and support, describe the relationship between illustrations and the story in which they appear. **1.7** Use illustrations and details in a story to describe its characters, setting, or events. **Range of Reading and Level of Text Complexity: K.10** Actively engage in group reading activities with purpose and understanding. **1.10** With prompting and support, read prose of appropriate complexity for grade 1. **INFORMATIONAL TEXT** **Key Ideas and Details: K.1** With prompting and support, ask and answer questions about key details in a text. **K.3** With prompting and support, describe the connection between two individuals, events, ideas, or pieces of information in a text. **1.1** Ask and answer questions about key details in a text. **1.3** Describe the connection between two individuals, events, ideas, or pieces of information in a text. **Craft and Structure: 1.6** Distinguish between information provided by pictures or other illustrations and information provided by other words in text. **Integration of Knowledge and Ideas: K.7** With prompting and support, describe the relationship between illustrations and the text in which they appear. **1.7** Use illustrations and details in a story to describe its key ideas. **Range of Reading and Level of Text Complexity: K.10** Actively engage in group reading activities with purpose and understanding. **1.10** With prompting and support, read informational texts appropriately complex for grade 1. **FOUNDATIONAL** **Print Concepts: K.1, 1.1** Demonstrate understanding of the organization and basic features of print. **Fluency: K.4** Read emergent-reader texts with purpose and understanding. **1.4** Read with sufficient accuracy and fluency to support comprehension.
Word Study • Hear initial consonants and medial short vowels	**FOUNDATIONAL** **Phonological Awareness: K.2, 1.2** Demonstrate understanding of spoken words, syllables, and sounds (phonemes). **Phonics and Word Recognition: K.3, 1.3** Know and apply grade-level phonics and word analysis skills in decoding words.
Guided Writing • Hear and record sounds, conventions, language	**FOUNDATIONAL** **Phonological Awareness: K.2, 1.2** Demonstrate understanding of spoken words, syllables, and sounds (phonemes). **Phonics and Word Recognition: K.3, 1.3** Know and apply grade-level phonics and word analysis skills in decoding words. **WRITING** **Text Types and Purposes: K.3** Use a combination of drawing, dictating, and writing to narrate a single event or several loosely linked events, tell about the events in the order in which they occurred, and provide a reaction to what happened. **1.3** Write narratives in which they recount two or more appropriately sequenced events, include some details regarding what happened, use temporal words to signal event order, and provide some sense of closure.

*The Common Core State Standards are used here as a point of reference.

Emergent Guided Reading Lesson Plan

Title: _____ Level: _____ Lesson #:_____

Day 1 Date: _____	**Day 2** Date: _____
Sight Word Review—Writing _____ _____ _____	**Sight Word Review—Writing** _____ _____ _____
Introduce New Book: This book is called _____ and it's about _____ _____ **New vocabulary:**	**Rereading of Yesterday's Book (and other familiar books)** Observations:
Text Reading With Prompting: ☐ Check the picture. What would make sense? ☐ Get your mouth ready for the first sound. ☐ Get your mouth ready and check the picture. ☐ Could it be _____ or _____? ☐ Show me the word _____. ☐ Check the word with your finger. Are you right? ☐ Try reading without pointing. ☐ How would the character say that? (show expression)	
Teaching Points After Reading (choose one or two each day): ☐ One-to-one matching (at level C, discourage pointing) ☐ Use picture clues (meaning) ☐ Monitor with known words ☐ Get mouth ready for initial sound ☐ Cross-check picture and first letter ☐ Visual scanning (check the word left to right) ☐ Fluency and expression	
Discussion Prompt (if appropriate):	**Discussion Prompt (if appropriate):**
Teach One Sight Word: _____ • What's missing? • Table Writing • Mix & Fix • Writing on a whiteboard	**Teach Same Sight Word:** _____ • What's missing? • Table Writing • Mix & Fix • Writing on a whiteboard
Word Study (Choose just one): ☐ Picture sorts: _____ ☐ Making words: _____ ☐ Sound boxes: _____	**Guided Writing:** Dictated or open-ended sentence

TM ® & © Scholastic Inc. All rights reserved. *The Next Step in Guided Reading* copyright © 2009 by Jan Richardson. Published by Scholastic Inc.

Early Readers

The early guided reading lesson is primarily designed for first-grade readers. It is relatively common, however, for advanced kindergarten readers and challenged second and third graders to be reading at the early level. In this section, I'll demonstrate how to:

▶ Identify early readers
▶ Create a lesson plan for a small group of early readers
▶ Teach an early lesson based on the lesson plan
▶ Target key teaching points in the lesson

Profile of an Early Reader

Video Running Time: 2:33 | scholastic.com/NSGRActionK2

Take a moment to look at the overview below and then view "Profile of an Early Reader."

Who is an early reader? Early readers know the letters and their sounds, but they may still be learning how to apply these skills to attack challenging words. They should be able to read about 30–60 sight words; otherwise, they will struggle with fluency.

Text Reading at the Early Level

Early readers will read Levels D–I texts. As shown below, the specific text you choose will differ according to your focus.

Monitor and decode: Select a text at students' instructional level.

Fluency: Choose an easier text with dialogue.

Retelling: Select a fiction text with a clear problem and solution. When children reach Levels E and higher, the stories grow more complex and have several characters. Setting and plot become more important.

Be sensitive to ELLs' limited vocabularies. Choose texts with strong picture support, especially for unfamiliar concepts.

REFLECTION

After you view the video, reflect on the students in your classroom who may be at the early stage.

ACTION

▶ First assess your students. The most helpful assessment for analyzing early readers is a running record on a slightly challenging text. The running record will indicate the student's instructional level, reveal the cues and strategies he or she uses, and provide valuable information on decoding skills, fluency, and ability to retell. Record this information on the Assessment Summary Chart for Early Readers (Levels D–I) to help you form groups according to their needs. For more information on how to fill in the chart, see "Directions for Using the Assessment Summary Chart for Early Readers." (Forms available online)

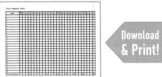

▶ Use the Class Progress Chart to track the progress of your early readers as they move from one stage to the next. (Form available online) Although children will differ in their rate of acceleration, the average progress for early readers is one level per month.

The chart below shows the skills children will learn as they progress through the early reading levels.

Early Reading Skills

- Monitor by checking the meaning of the story and scanning the word for a visual match.
- Problem-solve new words using a variety of strategies.
- Reread at points of difficulty to access meaning and structure.
- Read with fluency, phrasing, and expression.
- Make predictions.
- Remember and retell what they have read.
- Read and write a large bank of sight words.
- During reading and writing, apply phonetic principles, such as blends, vowel combinations, the silent-e rule, and endings.

Early Guided Reading Lesson Plan: Step by Step

Video Running Time: 9:49 | *scholastic.com/NSGRActionK2*

In this video, I explain how to plan and teach an early guided reading lesson. Before you view the video, take a moment to look at the Early Lesson Framework below.

What does the early guided reading lesson framework look like? The chart below shows the components of an early guided reading lesson like the one I teach in the video.

Early Lesson Framework

DAY 1: Lesson Component	DAY 2: Lesson Component
Before Reading Sight Word Review—Writing *(1 min)*	Sight Word Review—Writing *(1 min)*
Introduce New Book: Title/Gist New Vocabulary *(3–4 min)*	Continue Reading Yesterday's Book (and other familiar books) *(5–8 min)*
Read & Respond Text Reading With Prompting *(8–10 min)*	Text Reading With Prompting *(8–10 min)*
Teaching Points After Reading *(1–2 min)*	Teaching Points After Reading *(1–2 min)*
Discussion Prompt *(1–2 min)*	Discussion Prompt *(1–2 min)*
After Reading Teach One Sight Word *(1 min)*	Teach Same Sight Word *(1 min)*
Word Study *(5–8 min)*	Guided Writing *(8–10 min)*

MANAGEMENT TIPS! For an in-depth explanation of the procedures for an early guided reading lesson, see "Description of Early Guided Reading Lesson (Two-Day Plan)" on pages 116–133 of *The Next Step in Guided Reading*. (pages 120–146 of *The Next Step Forward in Guided Reading*)

TEACHING AN INDIVIDUAL EARLY READER There are occasions when you may want to do an individual guided reading lesson because a particular student does not fit into any group. This is often a short-term problem since groupings change frequently. For information on teaching an individual early lesson, see "Ten-Minute Lesson for Early Readers (Individual Instruction)" on the website.

TIME FRAME FOR AN EARLY GUIDED READING LESSON Allot 20 minutes for a lesson. Using a timer and limiting teacher talk will help you transition between activities every few minutes—and keep your students engaged and focused.

THE EARLY GUIDED READING GROUP Group students together who are reading no more than one level apart. Most students reading at the early levels need more work on decoding skills and fluency, but some may need to focus on retelling or monitoring for meaning. Although you will have a single lesson focus, you can use prompts during reading to meet the diverse needs of your students. Find a list of prompts and teaching points online.

Download & Print!

Continue to update your Assessment Summary Chart monthly. Use the information to regroup students for guided reading.

REFLECTION

View "Early Guided Reading Lesson Plan: Step by Step" and reflect on the needs of the students in your classroom. Consider how you will group your students. Then, think about the lesson for each group.

▸ *Which sight words will you review?*

▸ *Which text would be appropriate for the group?*

▸ *How will you introduce this text?*

▸ *Does the text contain some known sight words and the sight word you will introduce?*

▸ *Which word study activity would be the best option for teaching phonics skills?*

▸ *How will you have students respond to the text during guided writing?*

SELF-MONITORING Self-monitoring is the foundation of comprehension. It is extremely important that children listen to themselves as they read and stop if what they say does not make sense. When you ask a child, "Does that make sense?" you are teaching the foundation of comprehension.

ACTION

▸ Complete an Assessment Summary Chart for Early Readers (Levels D–I) for a group. (Form available online)

▸ Use your completed chart to ensure that your groupings meet your students' needs.

Download & Print!

Download & Print!

▸ Now it's time to fill out your own lesson plan. Use the Early Guided Reading Lesson Plan on page 43 to design a lesson plan for one group that you've targeted.

▸ Review my explanation of each lesson component in the video as you work. Additional information appears on the next page.

① SIGHT WORD REVIEW—WRITING

Dictate three known sight words for students to write.

② INTRODUCE NEW BOOK

Keeping your focus strategy in mind, select a book whose story makes sense, contains a problem and a solution, and has strong picture support. Identify words that may be difficult to decode.

③ TEXT READING WITH PROMPTING

On Day 1, students begin to read the book independently with prompting from you. On Day 2, they finish the book and reread it. If students finish reading the book on Day 1, they can reread it and other familiar books on Day 2. As you monitor reading, focus on the target strategy but differentiate your instruction to meet each student's needs.

④ TEACHING POINTS AFTER READING

Select one or two examples from the story to demonstrate a specific strategy. Ask yourself, "What do these students need to learn next?"

⑤ DISCUSSION PROMPTS

Prepare one question each day that requires students to make inferences or draw conclusions about the story.

⑥ TEACH ONE SIGHT WORD

On Day 1, introduce a new sight word from the book. Use all four activities in sequence to teach the word. On Day 2, review the word using all four activities again. Once students learn to write about 50–60 sight words, you can omit this component.

⑦ WORD STUDY

Do one activity that matches students' decoding/phonics needs.

⑧ GUIDED WRITING

Have students write a short response to the book: at Levels D and E, students write dictated sentences or complete open-ended sentences; at Levels F–I, they could write about the beginning, middle, and end, the problem and solution, or a one-sentence summary based on the Somebody-Wanted-But-So (S-W-B-S) framework. If students read an informational book, prompt them to write about something they learned.

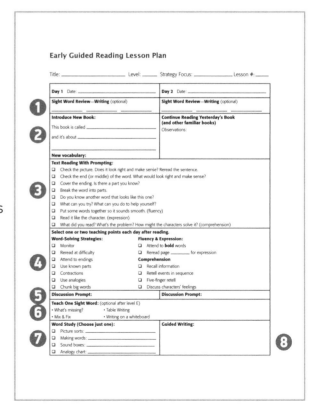

Materials You Will Need for the Early Lesson

For each group, gather the following materials:

- Dry-erase boards, markers, and erasers (1 for each student and 1 for you)
- Sets of lowercase magnetic letters (6–8 sets)
- Pictures for sound sorts (short medial vowels, digraphs, and initial blends)
- Guided writing journals with lined paper (1 for each student)
- Assessment kit, which includes leveled reading passages, comprehension questions, and a word knowledge inventory
- Leveled books (D–I)
- Early Guided Reading Lesson Plan (several copies): A reproducible appears on page 43.
- High-Frequency Word Chart for Levels C–E (1 for each group): Use the information on this chart to select guided reading books, plan your word study, and create your dictated sentences for guided writing. (Form available online)
- Sound Box/Analogy Template (place in a heavy plastic sheet protector): Students will use this template for segmenting words during word study. (Form available online)
- Timer

SOME COMMONLY ASKED QUESTIONS

How do I select my teaching points? Remember to record student miscues during reading and circle those that might be corrected by a teaching point. You will have only a few seconds to decide the best teaching point for the group. Limit yourself to two teaching points and teach by demonstration. Begin a teaching point by saying, "Let me show you something." That will automatically shift you into the demonstration mode. You will most commonly work on decoding strategies because decoding is the greatest challenge for early readers, but sometimes fluency and/or comprehension are appropriate to teach on Day 2.

What should I do if I have to put students who read at different levels in the same group? It is common to group students with adjacent reading levels. For example, students reading at Level G can be grouped with children reading at Level H. Sometimes it is necessary to group students who are reading more than one level apart so you can reduce the number of groups in your classroom. If you have to put a few students reading at Level F with one or two students reading at Level H, match the texts to the readers and introduce one book each day. For example, on Monday introduce a new book to the Level F group; students at Level H read familiar books they have read in previous guided reading lessons. Listen to each child and prompt for appropriate strategies. All students would do the same word study activity. On Tuesday, introduce a new book to the Level H group; the students at Level F will reread Monday's new book and other familiar books. Then all students would do a guided writing activity related to the new book they have read.

Model Lesson in Action: Early Reader

Video Running Time: 21:17 | scholastic.com/NSGRActionK2

In this video, I show what an early lesson at Level D/E looks and sounds like. The group is composed of three first graders, two of whom are English language learners. Although students understand the essence of a story, their decoding and fluency skills are weak. I chose the book *A Hungry Puppy* by Michèle Dufresne because the story has a beginning, middle, and end, as well as engaging photographs that provide strong support for the text.

VIEW ONLINE Take a moment to look at the completed lesson plan with my observations below and then view the video. I suggest you download and print the completed Early Guided Reading Lesson Plan and refer to it as you watch the lesson.

Early Guided Reading Lesson Plan

Title: *A Hungry Puppy*   Level: *D/E*   Strategy Focus: *Reading for Meaning*   Lesson #: _____

Day 1 Date: _____ | **Day 2** Date: _____

Before Reading

Sight Word Review—Writing (optional)
look   here   said

Introduce New Book:
This book is called *A Hungry Puppy*
and it's about *a little puppy who is hungry and looks for food to eat. Read to find out if Bella + Rosie share their food.*
Oh thank you (p12)
New vocabulary: *woof (p2) away (p6) cried (p11)*

Sight Word Review—Writing (optional)
went   come   get

Continue Reading Yesterday's Book
(and other familiar books)
Observations: *Prompt to reread at point of difficulty*
B- woof
m- cried
E- Oh Thank You
Good comprehension
Did well with retell using key words

Read & Respond

Text Reading With Prompting:
- ☒ Check the picture. Does it look right and make sense? Reread the sentence.
- ☐ Check the end (or middle) of the word. What would look right and make sense?
- ☐ Cover the ending. Is there a part you know?
- ☐ Break the word into parts.
- ☐ Do you know another word that looks like this one?
- ☐ What can you try? What can you do to help yourself?
- ☒ Put some words together so it sounds smooth. (fluency)
- ☐ Read it like the character. (expression)
- ☐ What did you read? What's the problem? How might the characters solve it? (comprehension)

Select one or two teaching points each day after reading.

Word-Solving Strategies:
- ☒ Monitor
- ☐ Reread at difficulty
- ☐ Attend to endings
- ☐ Use known parts
- ☐ Contractions
- ☐ Use analogies
- ☐ Chunk big words

Fluency & Expression:
- ☐ Attend to **bold** words
- ☒ Reread page *10-12* for expression

Comprehension
- ☐ Recall information
- ☒ Retell events in sequence   *Discuss beginning-middle-end*
- ☐ Five-finger retell
- ☐ Discuss characters' feelings

Discussion Prompt: *Why doesn't Rosie want to share her food?*
Discussion Prompt: *Why do Bella + Rosie decide to share their food?*

After Reading

Teach One Sight Word: (optional after level E)
- • What's missing?   • Table Writing
- • Mix & Fix   • Writing on a whiteboard

went   maybe one more day on this word

Word Study (Choose just one):
- ☐ Picture sorts: _____
- ☒ Making words: *Sat, mat, math, bath, bash, mash*
- ☐ Sound boxes: _____
- ☐ Analogy chart: _____

too hard - use picture sorts

Guided Writing:
The puppy went to get some food.
TP= use lower case letters.
Excellent Independence - stretched out words.

DAY 1

BEFORE READING

SIGHT WORD REVIEW–WRITING I spend a minute at the beginning of the lesson reviewing three sight words from previous guided reading lessons. As I dictate each word, students write it on their whiteboards. It's best to intervene while the student is writing rather than allowing him or her to write the word incorrectly. Put a checkmark on the High-Frequency Word Chart if a student is able to write the word without support. Students should have at least six checkmarks for each word before you stop reviewing it. You can omit this component once students know how to write 50–60 sight words.

INTRODUCE NEW BOOK AND VOCABULARY

Gist Statement: State the title and briefly tell about the story; include the names of the characters and a short description of the problem.

Text Preview and New Vocabulary: Before they read, students should look through the book and use the pictures to construct the meaning of the story. You do not need to discuss every page, but do attend to unfamiliar concepts and new sight words that students cannot decode. This is especially important for students who are learning English. Write the words on a whiteboard so they can see the unusual spelling. Say the word and have them repeat it. In my lesson plan, I used the new vocabulary from the beginning, middle, and end of the story.

READ & RESPOND

TEXT READING WITH PROMPTING Students whisper-read the book independently while you observe, prompt, coach, and teach individuals. Do not allow choral or round-robin reading. This inhibits problem-solving behaviors and creates dependent readers. And do not allow them to read silently. Reading aloud softly helps students monitor and recall what they read. As students read, differentiate instruction by deciding which prompt each one needs. Focus on these target strategies: self-monitoring, decoding, fluency, and comprehension.

Notice in the video how I prompted Mayrani to monitor her reading. On Day 2, I framed phrases with my fingers as individual students read, and I used the prompt, "Put some words together so it sounds smooth," to help develop their fluency.

TEACHING POINTS AFTER READING After students have read for 8–10 minutes, spend a few minutes teaching strategies for decoding, fluency and expression, and/or comprehension. Usually decoding is the teaching point for early readers, but sometimes fluency and/or comprehension are appropriate teaching points for Day 2. Regardless of your focus, always emphasize reading for meaning.

Target Skills and Strategies

For more information on the following skills and strategies, see the "Teaching Points" video clips:

- Decode With Known Parts: Write a tricky word on a whiteboard and show students how to separate a word into known and unknown parts, as I did with the word *farmer*: *farm + er*.

- Read With Fluency: Select one or two pages for a student to read aloud with your support. Fluency improves as students build automaticity with sight words and decoding strategies.

- Reread at Point of Difficulty: Model going back and rereading if something doesn't sound right or make sense.

- Use Meaning to Decode a Word: Sometimes the simple prompt, "Think about the story," is enough, but you may need to scaffold with a more supportive prompt.

- Read With Expression: Create different voices for the characters as you read a fiction text.

- Make Inferences to Build Comprehension: Use a sample prompt to guide students to make inferences about the book and offer support as necessary.

DISCUSSION PROMPT To help students make inferences or draw conclusions about the story they've read, ask an open-ended question.

AFTER READING

TEACH ONE SIGHT WORD Teach one new sight word from the book to students at Levels D and E. Be sure to do all four activities—*What's Missing?*, *Mix & Fix*, *Table Writing*, and *Writing on a Whiteboard*—in sequence. Teaching a new sight word is optional for Level E students if they can write 50–60 words because these students have developed strong visual memory skills. They will continue to learn new words during reading, writing, and through your classroom spelling program. Remember to keep a record of their correct responses on the High-Frequency Word Chart.

WORD STUDY Students reading at Levels D–I are still learning phonics. Spend the last part of the Day 1 lesson doing one of the following word study activities that matches their decoding/phonics needs: picture sorts, making words, sound boxes, or analogy chart. Here is a list of skills to target for each level:

- ▶ **Level D:** digraphs, endings

- ▶ **Level E:** initial blends, onsets/rimes, contractions

- ▶ **Level F:** final blends, onsets/rimes, contractions

- ▶ **Level G:** blends, silent-*e* rule

- ▶ **Levels H–I:** vowel patterns, endings, compound words

DAY 2

Follow the same procedures as Day 1 for sight word review, reading text with prompting, and teaching points after reading. Have students finish reading the new book you introduced in Day 1.

GUIDED WRITING Writing a short response to the book helps students extend comprehension and apply phonetic principles you have taught during word study. Have them write their responses on the bottom half of their journals and, on the top, practice letter formation or work on unknown words with your help. In the video, I dictated a sentence to students since they were at Level D/E. I also worked on letter formation when I asked them to write the letter *p* in uppercase and lowercase.

As students write, you have the opportunity to differentiate your support to teach them the skills they need. It is likely you will use different teaching points for each writer in the group.

REFLECTION

Take time to evaluate my model lesson. Based on what you saw, would you make any changes in your lesson plan?

ACTION

- ▶ Complete the Rubric for Early Guided Reading Lesson (Levels D–I) to evaluate its components. (Form available online)

- ▶ Review and refine your lesson plan.

- ▶ Teach your lesson. Remember to use the notes and observations on your lesson plan to assess your students' performance and progress.

THE EARLY GUIDED READING LESSON FRAMEWORK: ADDRESSING STANDARDS

The chart below shows how each component of the Early Lesson Framework aligns with commonly held state and national standards.

Early Lesson Component/ Objective	Standards*
Sight Word Review— Writing New Sight Word • High-frequency words	**FOUNDATIONAL** **Phonics and Word Recognition: 1.3** Know and apply grade-level phonics and word analysis skills in decoding words. *Also K.3*
Introduce New Book • Oral language • Print concepts	**LITERATURE** **Integration of Knowledge and Ideas: 1.7** Use illustrations and details in a story to describe its characters, setting, or events. *Also K.7, 2.7; FOUNDATIONAL: Print Concepts: K.1*
Text Reading With Prompting Discussion Prompt • Oral language • Comprehension	**LITERATURE/INFORMATIONAL TEXT** **Key Ideas and Details: 1.1** Ask and answer questions about key details in a text. *Also K.1, 2.1*
Word Study • Phonics	**FOUNDATIONAL** **Phonological Awareness: 1.2** Demonstrate understanding of spoken words, syllables, and sounds (phonemes). *Also K.2* **Phonics and Word Recognition: 1.3** Know and apply grade-level phonics and word analysis skills in decoding words. *Also K.3, 2.3*
Guided Writing • Respond to literature	**WRITING** **1.3** Write narratives in which they recount two or more appropriately sequenced events, including some details regarding what happened, using temporal words to signal event order, and providing some sense of closure. *Also 2.3*

*The Common Core State Standards are used here as a point of reference.

Early Guided Reading Lesson Plan

Title: _____ Level: _____ Strategy Focus: _____ Lesson #: _____

Day 1 Date: _____	**Day 2** Date: _____
Sight Word Review—Writing (optional) _____ _____ _____	**Sight Word Review—Writing** (optional) _____ _____ _____
Introduce New Book: This book is called _____ and it's about _____ **New vocabulary:**	**Continue Reading Yesterday's Book (and other familiar books)** Observations:

Text Reading With Prompting:

- ❑ Check the picture. Does it look right and make sense? Reread the sentence.
- ❑ Check the end (or middle) of the word. What would look right and make sense?
- ❑ Cover the ending. Is there a part you know?
- ❑ Break the word into parts.
- ❑ Do you know another word that looks like this one?
- ❑ What can you try? What can you do to help yourself?
- ❑ Put some words together so it sounds smooth. (fluency)
- ❑ Read it like the character. (expression)
- ❑ What did you read? What's the problem? How might the characters solve it? (comprehension)

Select one or two teaching points each day after reading.

Word-Solving Strategies:	**Fluency & Expression:**
❑ Monitor	❑ Attend to **bold** words
❑ Reread at difficulty	❑ Reread page _____ for expression
❑ Attend to endings	**Comprehension**
❑ Use known parts	❑ Recall information
❑ Contractions	❑ Retell events in sequence
❑ Use analogies	❑ Five-finger retell
❑ Chunk big words	❑ Discuss characters' feelings

Discussion Prompt:	**Discussion Prompt:**

Teach One Sight Word: (optional after level E)

• What's missing?	• Table Writing
• Mix & Fix	• Writing on a whiteboard

Word Study (Choose just one):	**Guided Writing:**
❑ Picture sorts: _____ ❑ Making words: _____ ❑ Sound boxes: _____ ❑ Analogy chart: _____	

TM ® & © Scholastic Inc. All rights reserved. *The Next Step in Guided Reading* copyright © 2009 by Jan Richardson. Published by Scholastic Inc.

Transitional Readers and Fluent Readers

It is common to find both transitional and fluent readers in the primary grades. To determine the reading stage of your students, consider grade level, text level, and instructional needs. The chart below will help you with this process.

General Guidelines for Identifying Transitional and Fluent Readers			
Grade	**Text Levels**	**Instructional Needs**	**Transitional or Fluent Guided Reading**
Kindergarten & First Grade	Above Level I	decoding, vocabulary, comprehension	Transitional
Second Grade	Levels J–M	decoding, fluency, vocabulary, retell	Transitional
Second Grade	Above Level M	vocabulary, comprehension	Fluent

In this section, I'll demonstrate how to:

▶ Identify transitional and fluent readers
▶ Create lesson plans for small groups of transitional and fluent readers
▶ Teach a transitional lesson based on the lesson plan
▶ Teach a fluent lesson based on the lesson plan
▶ Target key teaching points in the lessons

Profile of Transitional and Fluent Readers

Video Running Time: 2:53 | scholastic.com/NSGRActionK2

EW
INE Take a moment to look at the overview below and then view "Profile of Transitional and Fluent Readers."

Who is a transitional reader? Transitional readers need to work on one or more of the following areas: decoding multisyllabic words, increasing fluency, expanding vocabulary, or improving comprehension. Phonics skills taught at this level include complex vowels, the silent-*e* feature, and words with more than two syllables.

Who is a fluent reader? Fluent readers are good decoders, so they are able to explore the deeper levels of comprehension by reading challenging texts. The focus for fluent guided reading is using a variety of vocabulary and comprehension strategies.

Text Reading at the Transitional and the Fluent Levels

Transitional readers will read texts at Levels J–M, especially short fiction written specifically for guided reading.

Fluent readers may read any relatively short text—poetry, short stories, newspaper and magazine articles, short chapter books, informational books—as long as the text offers the right amount of challenge. You can also have fluent readers read a chapter from a novel to teach a particular strategy, such as foreshadowing, mood, or inferencing.

Encourage fluent readers to choose novels for self-selected reading and book clubs, but monitor their choices to make sure the text is at their independent level. The books should be one or two levels below their instructional level so they can read with fluency and a high degree of accuracy, and with minimal teacher support. Avoid reading entire novels during guided reading, as they take too long to read.

 SUPPORT YOUR FOCUS STRATEGY Your primary goal in choosing a text for readers at any stage is finding one that supports your focus strategy.

REFLECTION

After you view the video, reflect on the students in your classroom who may be at the transitional or the fluent stage.

Action

▶ First assess your students.

> **Transitional Readers:** I have found the following types of assessments most useful for analyzing the strengths and needs of transitional readers:
>
> • *Running record with comprehension questions:* A running record will help you select a text and a focus strategy for your lesson. Administer it to individual students to identify their instructional reading level, reading strategies, and comprehension abilities. Have them read aloud so you can record their reading behaviors.
>
> • *Word study inventory:* Administer a word study inventory to the entire class to assess phonics skills. The inventory will identify the specific skills you should teach during the word study and guided writing components of your lesson. There is a Word Study Inventory for Transitional Readers on the website.

Down & Pr

> **Fluent Readers:** Administer a running record with comprehension questions as you did with transitional readers, but have the fluent readers read the passage silently. To assess comprehension, ask each child to give you an oral retell and respond to some questions about the passage.

▶ Record information from the assessments on the appropriate assessment summary chart to help you form groups according to student needs. Use the Assessment Summary Chart for Transitional Readers or the Assessment Summary Chart for Fluent Readers. (Forms available online) For more information on how to fill in the charts, see the directions on the website.

Down & Pr

▶ Use the Class Progress Chart to track the progress of your readers as they move from one level to the next.

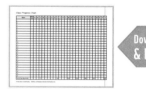

Down & Pr

Transitional and Fluent Guided Reading Lesson Plans: Step by Step

Video Running Time: 9:58 | scholastic.com/NSGRActionK2

In this video, I explain how to plan and teach a transitional and a fluent guided reading lesson. An overview of the transitional lesson appears below. The fluent lesson overview begins on page 50.

TRANSITIONAL LESSON PLAN

Before you view the video, take a moment to look at the Transitional Lesson Framework below.

What does the transitional lesson framework look like? The chart below shows the components of a transitional guided reading lesson like the one I teach on the video.

Transitional Lesson Framework	
DAY 1: Lesson Component	**DAY 2: Lesson Component**
Before Reading Gist statement introducing new book Preview text Teach new vocabulary *(3–4 min)*	**Before Reading** Preview next section Teach new vocabulary *(2–3 min)*
Read & Respond Text Reading With Prompting *(10–12 min)*	**Read & Respond** Continue Reading With Prompting *(10–12 min)*
Teaching Points *(1–2 min)*	Teaching Points *(1–2 min)*
Discussion Prompt *(1–2 min)*	Discussion Prompt *(1–2 min)*
After Reading Word Study *(3–5 min)*	**After Reading** Word Study *(3–5 min)*
DAY 3: Lesson Component Rereading for Fluency *(optional: 5 min)* Guided Writing *(15–20 min)*	

For an in-depth explanation of the procedures for a transitional guided reading lesson, see pages 157–172 of *The Next Step in Guided Reading* (pages 175–202 of *The Next Step Forward in Guided Reading*).

TEACHING AN INDIVIDUAL TRANSITIONAL READER If you have a transitional reader who does not fit into any of your guided reading groups, teach him or her individually for ten minutes each day until the student accelerates and is able to join a group. For information on teaching an individual transitional lesson, see "Ten-Minute Lesson for Transitional Readers (Individual Instruction)" on the website.

TIME FRAME FOR A TRANSITIONAL GUIDED READING LESSON
Allot about 20 minutes for a lesson. Using a timer and limiting teacher talk will help you pace your lesson and keep your students engaged and focused. It usually takes two or three days for transitional readers to finish a book.

THE TRANSITIONAL GUIDED READING GROUP Students one or two levels apart can be grouped together, but it's difficult to meet each student's needs if you have too many reading levels in one group. Transitional readers can be quite diverse. Some might have difficulty decoding but are able to recall; others may be fluent decoders but need to improve recall and retelling. The transitional lesson format provides for differentiated instruction because you can tailor your prompting and teaching points to individual students.

Continue to update your Assessment Summary Chart monthly and use the information to regroup students for guided reading. The average rate of progress for transitional students is one level every 8–9 weeks.

REFLECTION

View "Transitional/Fluent Lesson Plan: Step by Step" and reflect on the needs of the transitional students in your classroom. Consider how you will group them, then think about the lesson for each group.

> ▸ *Which transitional students are within one or two levels of each other?*

> ▸ *Which focus strategy will you use for each group?*

> ▸ *Which text supports the focus strategy?*

ACTION

> ▸ Complete an Assessment Summary Chart for Transitional Readers for a group. (Form available online)

> ▸ Use your completed chart to select a focus for your lesson.

> ▸ Now it's time to fill out your own lesson plan. Use the Transitional Guided Reading Lesson Plan on page 62 to design a lesson plan for the group you've targeted.

> ▸ Review my explanation of each lesson component in the video as you work. Additional information appears on the next page.

❶ INTRODUCE NEW BOOK/CONTINUE READING THE BOOK

For Day 1, prepare a gist statement for the book. Allow students a few minutes to preview the book and share their questions and/or predictions. Teach challenging words that students won't be able to decode on their own or that are not defined in the text.

❷ TEXT READING WITH PROMPTING

On Day 1, students begin to read the book independently with prompting from you. As you work with individual students, target your focus strategy but differentiate your prompting to meet each student's needs. On Day 2 (or Day 3), they finish the book.

❸ TEACHING POINTS

Refer to your anecdotal notes to choose one or two teaching points that match your students' needs.

❹ DISCUSSION PROMPT

Each day, prepare a question that requires students to make inferences or draw conclusions about the story.

❺ WORD STUDY

Do one activity that matches students' decoding/phonics needs. Use the Word Study Inventory and your observations to determine your focus. Not all transitional readers will need a word study activity.

❻ GUIDED WRITING

Choose one of the options to guide students to write a short response to the book.

Transitional Guided Reading Lesson Plan

Materials You Will Need for the Transitional Lesson

For each group, gather the following materials:

- Dry-erase board, marker, and eraser (for you)
- Sets of lowercase magnetic letters or letter cards for word study (6 sets)
- Guided writing journals or reading notebooks (1 for each student)
- Assessment kit, which includes leveled reading passages, comprehension questions, and a word knowledge inventory
- Leveled books J–M, especially short fiction and informational texts written specifically for guided reading
- Transitional Guided Reading Lesson Plan (several copies): A reproducible appears on page 62.
- Personal Word Wall for Guided Writing (6 copies). (Form available online)
- Sound Box Template/Analogy Chart (place in a heavy plastic sheet protector). Students will use this template for segmenting words during word study. (Form available online)
- Timer

FLUENT LESSON PLAN

Before you view the video, take a moment to look at the Fluent Lesson Framework below.

What does the fluent lesson framework look like? The chart below shows the components of a fluent guided reading lesson like the one I teach in the video.

Fluent Lesson Framework		
Before Reading	**Read & Respond**	**After Reading**
Gist statement	Model strategy	Discussion
Preview & predict	*(1–2 min) Day 1 only*	Teaching points
(2–3 min) Day 1 only	Conference with students as they read and respond	• Decoding
New vocabulary	*(10–12 min)*	• Vocabulary
(1–2 min)		• Comprehension: fiction, nonfiction, or poetry
		(5 min)
		Words for New Word List
		(1 min)
After Reading Entire Text: Guided Writing *(optional: 20 min)*		

For an in-depth explanation of the procedures for a fluent guided reading lesson, see pages 189–198 of *The Next Step in Guided Reading* (pages 235–250 of *The Next Step Forward in Guided Reading*).

THE FLUENT GUIDED READING GROUP The Assessment Summary Chart for Fluent Readers makes it easy to group students flexibly, based on the strategy focus. The bottom line is this: Know your students and teach them what they need to learn to become better readers. About once a month, reevaluate your groups by reviewing the anecdotal notes you've taken during guided reading lessons. I recommend you don't put more than six students in a group so you have time to confer with each one.

REFLECTION

View "Transitional/Fluent Guided Reading Lesson Plan: Step by Step" and reflect on the needs of the fluent students in your classroom. Consider how you will group them, then think about the lesson for each group.

▶ *Which fluent readers need work on the same skill and/or strategy?*

▶ *Which focus strategy will you use with each group?*

▶ *What genre would best support the focus strategy?*

▶ *What text in that genre would support the focus strategy?*

▶ *How many days will it take for the group to read the entire text?*

ACTION

- ▶ Complete an Assessment Summary Chart for Fluent Readers (Form available online)

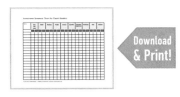

- ▶ Use your completed chart to ensure that your groupings meet your students' needs.

- ▶ Now it's time to fill out your own lesson plan. Use both pages of the Fluent Guided Reading Lesson Plan on pages 63–64 to design a lesson plan for one group that you've targeted.

- ▶ Review my explanation of each lesson component in the video as you work. Additional information appears below.

❶ BEFORE READING

Decide which sections of the text to read and discuss each day. For Day 1, prepare a gist statement that gives students a general overview of the text. Then help them preview the illustrations, headings, and other text features to make predictions and ask questions about what they will read. Model the focus strategy and introduce vocabulary that is not defined in the text.

❷ READ & RESPOND

Students begin to read the book independently with prompting from you. On subsequent days, they finish the book. As you monitor reading, focus on the target strategy but differentiate your instruction to meet each student's needs.

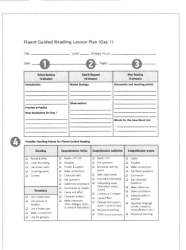

❸ AFTER READING

For each day of a lesson, write a thought-provoking question to lift the processing level of students.

❹ POSSIBLE TEACHING POINTS

Place a checkmark by the teaching points you want to use during and after reading.

❺ SUBSEQUENT DAYS

Repeat Day 1 procedures for the next sections of the text. Continue until the text is completed. You may then choose to do a Guided Writing activity to extend comprehension or support struggling writers. Some suggestions appear on the next page.

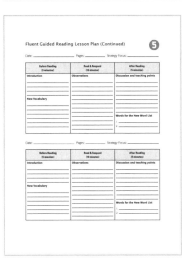

Guided Writing Activities for Fluent Readers

Fiction	Informational	Poetry
• Describe a character and give examples of his or her traits. • Write a poem from a character's point of view. • Explain a microtheme in the story. • Choose your own ending.	• Write a poem about a famous person. • Summarize a section of the book. • Use the index to find key ideas or two concepts to compare/contrast. • Write about the causes and effects of a historical event.	• Make connections to the poem. • Summarize the literal and figurative meanings of the poem. • Explain a literary element the poet used.

Materials You Will Need for the Fluent Lesson

For each group, gather the following materials:

- Dry-erase board, marker, and eraser (for you)
- Reading notebooks for student responses and new vocabulary (1 for each student)
- Assessment kit, which includes leveled reading passages and comprehension questions
- Texts in a variety of genres
- Fluent Guided Reading Lesson Plan (several copies): Reproducibles appear on pages 63–64.
- Sticky notes (1-inch and 3-inch) and sticky flags
- Timer

SOME COMMONLY ASKED QUESTIONS

What should I do while transitional students read at the table? You should have individual conferences with students based upon their needs. If a student has decoding and fluency issues, for instance, listen to him or her read and prompt accordingly. You can also listen to individual students as they retell a page, or engage them in a comprehension conversation.

What should I do while fluent students are reading silently? You should have mini-conferences with each student. Look at their written responses to select a focus for your conversation. Ask if there was something that confused them as they read. Pose a question about the text, or have students tell you what they are going to write next. You can also show them how to use vocabulary strategies. If you find that a student does not need any support, then the text is probably too easy or you need to change to a more challenging focus strategy.

Model Lesson in Action: Transitional Reader

Video Running Time: 23:07 | *scholastic.com/NSGRActionK2*

In this video, I show what a transitional lesson at Level J/K looks and sounds like. The group is composed of three second graders who are reading below grade level and need to improve their monitoring skills. I chose *The Great Gracie Chase* by Cynthia Rylant because the story is engaging and the illustrations support the plot and clarify challenging vocabulary.

Take a moment to look at the completed lesson plan below and then view the video. I suggest you download and print the completed Transitional Guided Reading Lesson Plan and refer to it as you watch the lesson.

Transitional Guided Reading Lesson Plan

Title: *The Great Gracie Chase* Level: **J/K** Strategy Focus: *monitor for meaning + decoding* Lesson #:_____

Before Reading

Day 1 Date_____ Pages_____
Introduce New Book: This book is about *a quiet, good dog named Gracie who decided to run away.*
New vocabulary: *p1- company* *p4- arrived* *p 7- clancy* *p11- naughty* *p 3- except*

Day 2 Date_____ Pages_____
Continue reading the book: You will read about *Gracie's adventures when she ran away.*
New vocabulary: *p 18- fountain* *p. 25- deliverywoman* *Text was slightly challenging for Gregory—able to decode words but only word-by-word.*

Read & Respond

Text Reading With Prompting (use prompts that target each student's needs)

Teaching Points: Choose one or two each day (decoding, vocabulary, fluency, and/or comprehension).

Decoding Strategies:
- ☒ Reread & think what would make sense
- ☐ Cover (or attend to) the ending
- ☐ Use analogies
- ☒ Chunk big words *decided*

Fluency & Phrasing: *p. 11*
- ☒ Phrasing
- ☒ Attend to **bold** words
- ☐ Attend to punctuation
- ☐ Dialogue, intonation & expression

Vocabulary Strategies:
- ☐ Reread the sentence and look for clues
- ☒ Check the picture *windowsill p 3*
- ☐ Use a known part
- ☐ Make a connection
- ☐ Use the glossary

Comprehension (oral):
- ☐ B-M-E ☐ Five-Finger Retell
- ☒ (S-W-B-S) ☐ Describe a character's feelings
- ☐ Who & What ☐ STP (Stop Think Paraphrase)
- ☐ Problem & Solution ☐ VIP (very important part)
- Other: *strong with comprehension*

Discussion Prompt: *Why did the painters put Gracie outside? Why didn't Gracie stop? good comprehension*

Discussion Prompt: *What caused Gracie to go back home?*

Word Study (if appropriate):
Sound boxes (Analogy chart) Make a big word *boat talk*

Word Study (if appropriate):
Sound boxes (Analogy chart) Make a big word *rain boat*

After Reading

Day 3 Date_____ **Reread the book for fluency (5 min) and/or engage in Guided Writing.**
Options for Guided Writing
Beginning-Middle-End   Five-Finger Retell   (Somebody-Wanted-But-So (SWBS))   Character Analysis
Problem/Solution   Compare or Contrast   Other:_____

Gracie wanted a quiet house but the painters were noisy so she ran away.

Before Reading

DAY 1: INTRODUCE NEW BOOK AND VOCABULARY

Gist Statement: Briefly tell about the book.

Text Preview and New Vocabulary: On Day 1, invite students to look through the book by studying the illustrations. You don't need to discuss every page, but do draw their attention to important information and unfamiliar concepts in the pictures. On subsequent days, students continue to read the text. Always introduce any words they will not be able to decode or define.

Read & Respond

TEXT READING WITH PROMPTING On each day of the lesson, students whisper-read the book independently while you confer with individuals. Prompt readers to monitor for meaning, decode, read fluently, and retell. Tailor your prompts to differentiate your instruction. In the video, for example, I praised Gregory for chunking his words. Then, to develop his fluency, I asked him to reread the paragraph.

TEACHING POINTS After students have read for 10–15 minutes, spend a few minutes teaching strategies for decoding, fluency and phrasing, vocabulary, and/or comprehension. Choose one or two teaching points each day based on the anecdotal notes you made during reading, and use the teaching points to elicit student responses to the text.

DISCUSSION PROMPT Ask a discussion prompt after each reading. On Day 1 of the model lesson, I asked, "Why did the painters put Gracie outside?" to guide students to make inferences about the story. Their answers gave me insight into their comprehension.

After Reading

WORD STUDY Each word study activity on the lesson plan is appropriate for teaching a specific phonics skill. Use sound boxes to teach short vowels, digraphs, and blends. Use analogy charts to practice the silent-*e* rule, vowel patterns, and inflectional endings. To teach students how to break apart multisyllabic words, give them magnetic letters or letter tiles to construct, break apart, and reconstruct a big word. On Day 1 of the model lesson, I used the analogy chart to work on the vowel patterns in *boat* and *talk* and to add endings. I pre-selected the words *walk(ed)*, *float(ed)*, and *cloak* to dictate to the students. The students in this group needed word study, but good spellers will not need this component.

REREADING FOR FLUENCY If your students need to improve fluency, allocate 5 minutes of the last day of the lesson to reread part of the book as you prompt individuals for fluency.

GUIDED WRITING This component occurs on the day after students finish reading the book. In this lesson, I planned for students to generate their own sentence using the "Somebody-Wanted-But-So" format. Guided Writing serves two purposes: to help them retell what they read and to improve their writing skills. This is guided writing, not assigned writing.

Target Skills and Strategies

For more information on the following skills and strategies, see the "Teaching Points" video clips:

- Make Inferences: Ask *why* questions to deepen students' thinking about the text.
- Reread With Fluency: Rereading a paragraph or two will help improve fluency.
- Make Connections to Known Words: Drawing an analogy to a known word can aid a student in decoding an unknown word.
- Introduce New Words in Four Steps: If there is no text support for determining a word's meaning, define the word, connect it to students' background, relate it to the text, and have them turn and talk about it.
- Neurological Impress With a Struggling Reader: Modulate your voice to support the student.

REFLECTION

Take time to evaluate my model lesson. Based on what you saw, would you make any changes in your lesson plan?

ACTION

▶ Complete the "Rubric for a Transitional Guided Reading Lesson (Levels J–P)" to evaluate its components. (Form available online)

▶ Review and refine your lesson plan.

▶ Teach your lesson. Remember to use the notes and observations on your lesson plan to assess your students' performance and progress.

THE TRANSITIONAL GUIDED READING LESSON FRAMEWORK: ADDRESSING STANDARDS

The chart below shows how each component of the Transitional Lesson Framework aligns with commonly held state and national standards.

Transitional Lesson Component/ Objective	Standards*
Introduce New Book Introduce Vocabulary • Oral language	**LITERATURE** **Integration of Knowledge and Ideas: 2.7** Use information gained from the illustrations and words in a print or digital text to demonstrate understanding of its characters, setting, or plot.

Text Reading With Prompting • Monitor for meaning • Decoding • Fluency • Retell **Teaching Points** • Decoding • Fluency & Phrasing • Vocabulary • Comprehension	**LITERATURE** **Key Ideas and Details: 2.1** Ask and answer such questions as who, what, where, when, why, and how to demonstrate understanding of key details in a text. *Also K.1, 1.1* **2.3** Describe how characters in a story respond to major events and challenges. *Also K.3, 1.3* **Craft and Structure: 2.6** Acknowledge differences in the points of view of characters, including by speaking in a different voice for each character when reading dialogue aloud. *Also 1.6* **Integration of Knowledge and Ideas: 2.7** Use information gained from the illustrations and words in a print text to demonstrate understanding of its characters, setting, and plot. *Also K.7, 1.7* **Range of Reading and Level of Text Complexity: 2.10** By the end of the year, read and comprehend literature, including stories and poetry, in the grades 2–3 complexity band proficiently, with scaffolding as needed at the high end of the range. *Also K.10, 1.10* **INFORMATIONAL TEXT** **Key Ideas and Details: 2.1** Ask and answer such questions as who, what, where, when, why, and how to demonstrate understanding of key details in a text. *Also K.1, 1.1* **2.3** Describe the connection between a series of historical events, scientific ideas or concepts, or steps in technical procedures in a text. *Also K.3, 1.3* **Craft and Structure: 2.4** Determine the meaning of words and phrases in a text relevant to a grade 2 topic or subject area. *Also K.4, 1.4* **2.6** Identify the main purpose of a text, including what the author wants to answer, explain, or describe. *Also 1.6* **Integration of Knowledge and Ideas: 2.8** Describe how reasons support specific points the author wants to make. *Also K.8, 1.8* **Range of Reading and Level of Text Complexity: 2.10** By the end of the year, read and comprehend informational texts, including history/social studies, science, and technical texts, in the grades 2–3 complexity band proficiently, with scaffolding as needed at the high end of the range. *Also K.10, 1.10* **FOUNDATIONAL** **Print Concepts: K.1, 1.1 Fluency: 2.4** Read with sufficient accuracy and fluency to support comprehension. *Also K.4, 1.4*
Discussion Prompt • Oral language • Comprehension	**LITERATURE** **Key Ideas and Details: 2.1** Ask and answer such questions as who, what, where, when, why, and how to demonstrate understanding of key details in a text. *Also K.1, 1.1*
Word Study • Phonics	**FOUNDATIONAL** **Phonics and Word Recognition: 2.3** Know and apply grade-level phonics and word analysis skills in decoding words. *Also Phonics and Word Recognition: K.3, 1.3; Phonological Awareness: K.2, 1.2*
Guided Writing • Respond to literature	**WRITING** **Text Types and Purposes: 2.3** Write narratives in which they recount a well-elaborated event or short sequence of events; include details to describe actions, thoughts, and feelings; use temporal words to signal event order; and provide a sense of closure. *Also 1.3*

*The Common Core State Standards are used here as a point of reference.

Model Lesson in Action: Fluent Reader

Video Running Time: 24:08 | scholastic.com/NSGRActionK2

In this video, I show what a fluent lesson looks and sounds like. The group is composed of four second graders who have just moved into a fluent guided reading group. I chose the book *Polar Bears* by Michèle Dufresne. Students have studied the Arctic, so they may be able to tap into their prior knowledge, and they have learned about a table of contents.

Take a moment to look at the completed lesson plan with my observations below and then view the video. I suggest you download and print the completed Fluent Guided Reading Lesson Plan and refer to it as you watch the lesson.

Fluent Guided Reading Lesson Plan (Day 1)

Title: *Polar Bears*   Level: M/N   Strategy Focus: Summarize

Date: _____   Pages: 1-8

Before Reading (5 minutes)	Read & Respond (10 minutes)	After Reading (5 minutes)
Introduction This book is about how polar bears survive in the Arctic + why they are a threatened species. RTFO interesting facts about polar bears. **Preview & Predict** Use Table of Contents **New Vocabulary for Day 1** p16 - transparent - clear p7- traction - grip	**Model Strategy** p4- Key words: cold, swimmers p6-camouflage,carnivore p7- small, feet p8- Arctic **Observations** Good decoders, fluent readers. Needed first letters to select key words. Good job with oral summary.	**Discussion and teaching points** Use the key words on each page to summarize the most important ideas from Chapter 1. Mad minute: Use some of the key words to write something new you learned/read about polar bears **Words for the New Word List** 1. transparent 2. traction (needed support)

Possible Teaching Points for Fluent Guided Reading

Decoding	Comprehension—fiction	Comprehension—n...
☐ Reread & think	☐ Retell—STP, VIP	☐ Retell—STP
☐ Cover the ending	☐ Visualize	☐ Ask questions
☐ Use known parts	☐ Predict & support	☒ Summarize w... words
☐ Chunk big words	☐ Make connections	☐ Main Idea/De...
☐ Connect	☐ Character traits	☐ Important/Int...
	☐ Ask questions	☐ Interpreting vi... information (... charts)
	☐ Determine importance	
Vocabulary	☐ Summarize by chapter	☐ Contrast or C...
	☐ Cause and effect	
☒ Use context clues	☐ Character analysis	☐ Cause/Effect
☐ Use pictures or visualize	☐ Make inferences— (from dialogue, action, or physical description	☐ Evaluate—fact/... author's point...
☐ Use a known part		☐ Reciprocal tea...
☐ Make a connection		☐ Other...
☒ Use the glossary		

Fluent Guided Reading Lesson Plan (Continued)

Date: _____   Pages: 8-17   Strategy Focus: Summarize

Before Reading (5 minutes)	Read & Respond (10 minutes)	After Reading (5 minutes)
Introduction Today you will read to find out more interesting facts about polar bears. Quickly preview Ch. 3,4. What questions are you asking yourself? **New Vocabulary** p12 rodent p16 crouches	**Observations** Scaffolds: Key words— Habitat - Arctic, ice floes Diet - seals, birds, fish, plants Hunt - holes, ice, crouch - Prompted them to use the glossary for both words - Found key words with little support. Next step - Students find key words without the support of initial letters	**Discussion and teaching points** Teach vocabulary strategies: - use context clues - ice floes p.8 - glossary - exhales p.15 Use key words to summarize - Ch 3 do orally, Ch 4 - do written (mad minute) **Words for the New Word List** 1. crouches 2. exhales

Date: _____   Pages: _____   Strategy Focus: _____

Before Reading (5 minutes)	Read & Respond (10 minutes)	After Reading (5 minutes)
Introduction _____ **New Vocabulary** _____	**Observations** _____	**Discussion and teaching points** _____ **Words for the New Word List** 1. 2.

BEFORE READING

INTRODUCE NEW BOOK

Gist Statement On Day 1, briefly explain what the book is about. On subsequent days, give a short statement about the next section students will read.

Preview & Predict Before they read on Day 1, have students look through the text and use the illustrations or table of contents to ask questions and make predictions about what they will read. In the model lesson, I had them use the table of contents and illustrations to predict new facts they might learn about polar bears.

New Vocabulary On each day of the lesson, introduce new vocabulary for the assigned section. Use the four steps of define, connect, relate the word to the text, and turn and talk, as I did in the lesson with the word *traction*. Notice, too, how I encouraged students to look up boldface words in the glossary if the word was unfamiliar.

 VOCABULARY

It's not necessary to introduce every new word. Bring a word to students' attention if

▶ they lack the decoding skills to read it (e.g., foreign words, proper names),

▶ they have never heard the word before,

▶ there are no clues about its meaning in the text,

▶ or the word is essential to understanding the passage.

READ & RESPOND

DAY 1: MODEL THE FOCUS STRATEGY On the first day of the lesson, model the focus strategy. Decide how you will scaffold your students as they practice the strategy. As they become more proficient in using the strategy, decrease your support. In the model lesson, I helped children find the most important words on each page by writing the first letter of each key word on a sticky note.

Students read the text independently, and silently, and write short responses that match the comprehension or vocabulary strategy. Writing during reading helps them organize their thoughts and keeps them focused on the task. Their written responses help you, too, for you can monitor their comprehension and see when to scaffold and support. While the group reads and responds, work with individuals. Prompt for vocabulary and comprehension during these mini-conferences. Record your observations to help you select teaching points to match the group's needs.

AFTER READING

DISCUSSION AND TEACHING POINTS After students have read for about 10 minutes, spend a few minutes discussing the text and focusing on comprehension and vocabulary teaching points. In the model lesson, students used the key words on their sticky notes to fashion a summary of each page in the book. We also checked to see if our initial predictions about the book were correct. As students took turns summarizing, I wove in teaching points about using the glossary and identifying the new vocabulary word.

WORDS FOR THE NEW WORD LIST Close each lesson by having students add two words on the New Word List in their reading notebooks. Select high-utility words or words that provide opportunities to teach word analysis strategies. In my model lesson, I chose the two new vocabulary words I introduced before reading, *transparent* and *traction*, because I expected they would encounter these words during content instruction and independent reading.

GUIDED WRITING During guided reading, students should always write short responses that match the comprehension focus. Some fluent readers struggle with writing; if your students need extra writing support, do a guided writing lesson the day after they finish reading the text. This writing activity should be completed with teacher support.

Target Skills and Strategies

For more information on the following skills and strategies, see the "Teaching Points" video clips:

- Revisit Predictions to Support Retell: Comparing what they thought they knew to what they learned by reading will help students recall information.

- Use Key Words to Summarize: Support students by giving clues to key words so they can use these words in their oral and written summaries.

- Introduce New Words in Four Steps: When a word doesn't have text support to help students determine its meaning, you should define it, connect it to their experiences, relate it to the text, and have them turn and talk about it.

REFLECTION

Take time to evaluate my model lesson. Based on what you saw, would you make any changes in your lesson plan?

ACTION

▸ Complete the Rubric for Fluent Guided Reading Lesson to evaluate its components. (Form available online)

▸ Review and refine your lesson plan.

▸ Teach your lesson. Remember to use the notes and observations on your lesson plan to assess your students' performance and progress.

THE FLUENT GUIDED READING LESSON FRAMEWORK: ADDRESSING STANDARDS

The chart below shows how each component of the Fluent Lesson Framework aligns with commonly held state and national standards.

Fluent Lesson Component/ Objective	Standards*
Introduce New Book • Oral language Preview & Predict New Vocabulary	**LITERATURE** **Integration of Knowledge and Ideas: 2.7** Use information gained from the illustrations and words in a print or digital text to demonstrate understanding of its characters, setting, or plot.
Model Strategy • Comprehension • Vocabulary Discussion and Teaching Points • Comprehension • Vocabulary	**LITERATURE** **Key Ideas and Details: 2.1** Ask and answer such questions as who, what, where, when, why, and how to demonstrate understanding of key details in a text. **2.3** Describe how characters in a story respond to major events and challenges. **Craft and Structure: 2.6** Acknowledge differences in the points of view of characters, including by speaking in a different voice for each character when reading dialogue aloud. **Integration of Knowledge and Ideas: 2.7** Use information gained from the illustrations and words in a print or digital text to demonstrate understanding of its characters, setting, and plot. **Range of Reading and Level of Text Complexity: 2.10** By the end of the year, read and comprehend literature, including stories and poetry, in the grades 2–3 complexity band proficiently, with scaffolding as needed at the high end of the range. **INFORMATIONAL TEXT** **Key Ideas and Details: 2.1** Ask and answer such questions as who, what, where, when, why, and how to demonstrate understanding of key details in a text. **2.2** Identify the main topic of a multiparagraph text as well as the focus of specific paragraphs within the text. **2.3** Describe the connection between a series of historical events, scientific ideas or concepts, or steps in technical procedures in a text. **Craft and Structure: 2.4** Determine the meaning of words and phrases in a text relevant to a grade 2 topic or subject area. **2.5** Know and use various text features (e.g., captions, bold print, subheadings, glossaries, indexes, electronic menus, icons) to locate key facts or information in a text efficiently. **2.6** Identify the main purpose of a text, including what the author wants to answer, explain, or describe. **Integration of Knowledge and Ideas: 2.8** Describe how reasons support specific points the author wants to make. **Range of Reading and Level of Text Complexity: 2.10** By the end of the year, read and comprehend informational texts, including history/social studies, science, and technical texts, in the grades 2–3 complexity band proficiently, with scaffolding as needed at the high end of the range. **FOUNDATIONAL** **Fluency: 2.4** Read with sufficient accuracy and fluency to support comprehension.
Words for New Word List • Phonics	**FOUNDATIONAL** **Phonics and Word Recognition: 2.3** Know and apply grade-level phonics and word analysis skills in decoding words.
Guided Writing • Respond to literature	**WRITING** **Text Types and Purposes: 2.3** Write narratives in which they recount a well-elaborated event or short sequence of events, include details to describe actions, thoughts, and feelings; use temporal words to signal event order, and provide a sense of closure. *Also 2.2*

*The Common Core State Standards are used here as a point of reference.

Transitional Guided Reading Lesson Plan

Title: _____ Level: _____ Strategy Focus: _____ Lesson #: _____

Day 1 Date_____ Pages_____	**Day 2** Date_____ Pages_____
Introduce New Book: This book is about _____ _____ **New vocabulary:**	**Continue reading the book:** You will read about _____ _____ **New vocabulary:**

Text Reading With Prompting (use prompts that target each student's needs)

Teaching Points: Choose one or two each day (decoding, vocabulary, fluency, and/or comprehension).

Decoding Strategies:	**Fluency & Phrasing:**
☐ Reread & think what would make sense	☐ Phrasing
☐ Cover (or attend to) the ending	☐ Attend to **bold** words
☐ Use analogies	☐ Attend to punctuation
☐ Chunk big words	☐ Dialogue, intonation & expression

Vocabulary Strategies:	**Comprehension (oral):**	
☐ Reread the sentence and look for clues	☐ B-M-E	☐ Five-Finger Retell
☐ Check the picture	☐ S-W-B-S	☐ Describe a character's feelings
☐ Use a known part	☐ Who & What	☐ STP (Stop Think Paraphrase)
☐ Make a connection	☐ Problem & Solution	☐ VIP (very important part)
☐ Use the glossary	Other:	

Discussion Prompt:	**Discussion Prompt:**

Word Study (if appropriate): Sound boxes–Analogy chart–Make a big word	**Word Study (if appropriate):** Sound boxes–Analogy chart–Make a big word

Day 3 Date_____ **Reread the book for fluency (5 min) and/or engage in Guided Writing.**
Options for Guided Writing

Beginning-Middle-End	Five-Finger Retell	Somebody-Wanted-But-So (SWBS)	Character Analysis
Problem/Solution	Compare or Contrast	Other: _____	

TM ® & © Scholastic Inc. All rights reserved. *The Next Step in Guided Reading* copyright © 2009 by Jan Richardson. Published by Scholastic Inc.

Fluent Guided Reading Lesson Plan (Day 1)

Title: _____ Level: _____ Strategy Focus: _____

Date: _____ Pages: _____

Before Reading (5 minutes)	Read & Respond (10 minutes)	After Reading (5 minutes)
Introduction _____ _____ _____ _____ **Preview & Predict** **New Vocabulary for Day 1** _____ _____ _____ _____	**Model Strategy** _____ _____ **Observations** _____ _____ _____ _____ _____ _____	**Discussion and teaching points** _____ _____ _____ _____ _____ _____ **Words for the New Word List** 1. _____ 2. _____

Possible Teaching Points for Fluent Guided Reading

Decoding	Comprehension–fiction	Comprehension–nonfiction	Comprehension–poetry
❑ Reread & think ❑ Cover the ending ❑ Use known parts ❑ Chunk big words ❑ Connect	❑ Retell—STP, VIP ❑ Visualize ❑ Predict & support ❑ Make connections ❑ Character traits ❑ Ask questions ❑ Determine importance ❑ Summarize by chapter ❑ Cause and effect ❑ Character analysis ❑ Make inferences (from dialogue, action, or physical description)	❑ Retell—STP ❑ Ask questions ❑ Summarize with key words ❑ Main Idea/Details ❑ Important/Interesting ❑ Interpreting visual information (maps, charts) ❑ Contrast or Compare ❑ Cause/Effect ❑ Evaluate fact/opinion, author's point of view ❑ Reciprocal teaching ❑ Other:_____	❑ Clarify ❑ Visualize ❑ Make connections ❑ Ask literal questions ❑ Summarize ❑ Ask inferential questions ❑ Make inferences ❑ Draw conclusions ❑ Interpret author's purpose ❑ Figurative language (simile, metaphor, personification, etc.) ❑ Reciprocal teaching
Vocabulary ❑ Use context clues ❑ Use pictures or visualize ❑ Use a known part ❑ Make a connection ❑ Use the glossary			

TM ® & © Scholastic Inc. All rights reserved. *The Next Step in Guided Reading* copyright © 2009 by Jan Richardson. Published by Scholastic Inc.

Fluent Guided Reading Lesson Plan (Continued)

Date: _____ Pages: _____ Strategy Focus: _____

Before Reading (5 minutes)	Read & Respond (10 minutes)	After Reading (5 minutes)
Introduction _____ _____ _____ **New Vocabulary** _____ _____ _____ _____ _____	**Observations** _____ _____ _____ _____ _____ _____ _____ _____ _____ _____ _____	**Discussion and teaching points** _____ _____ _____ _____ _____ _____ _____ **Words for the New Word List** 1. _____ 2. _____

Date: _____ Pages: _____ Strategy Focus: _____

Before Reading (5 minutes)	Read & Respond (10 minutes)	After Reading (5 minutes)
Introduction _____ _____ _____ **New Vocabulary** _____ _____ _____ _____ _____	**Observations** _____ _____ _____ _____ _____ _____ _____ _____ _____ _____ _____	**Discussion and teaching points** _____ _____ _____ _____ _____ _____ _____ **Words for the New Word List** 1. _____ 2. _____

TM ® & © Scholastic Inc. All rights reserved. *The Next Step in Guided Reading* copyright © 2009 by Jan Richardson. Published by Scholastic Inc.